POLICING THE FUTURE

13th European Policing Executive Conference
International Association of Chiefs of Police

edited by

A.B. Hoogenboom
M.J. Meiboom
D.C.M. Schoneveld
J.W.M. Stoop

1997
KLUWER LAW INTERNATIONAL
THE HAGUE – LONDON – BOSTON

Published by Kluwer Law International
P.O. Box 85889
2508 CN The Hague, The Netherlands

Sold and distributed in the USA and Canada by
Kluwer Law International
675 Massachusetts Avenue
Cambridge, MA 02139, USA

Sold and distributed in all other countries by
Kluwer Law International
Distribution Centre
P.O. Box 322
3300 AH Dordrecht, The Netherlands

Library of Congress Cataloging-in-Publication Data is available from the Library of Congress

Cover photo: Stichting VVV Rotterdam
Printed on acid-free paper

ISBN: 90 411 0416 X

© 1997, Kluwer Law International

Kluwer Law International incorporates the publishing programmes of Graham & Trotman Ltd, Kluwer Law and Taxation Publishers and Martinus Nijhoff Publishers.

POLICING THE FUTURE

ONE WEEK LOAN

A fine will be charged if kept beyond date stamped above

10013

TABLE OF CONTENTS

PREFACE

B. Hoogenboom and M.J. Meiboom

The International Association of Chiefs of Police (IACP) has about 15,000 high-ranking police officers from 82 different countries as its members. The Thirteenth IACP Conference 'Policing the Future', hosted by the Rotterdam-Rijnmond Regional Police, can be characterised by its multi-disciplinary approach towards law enforcement development.

Between 12 and 14 May 1996, police officials from around the world met in Rotterdam (the Netherlands) to discuss the future of policing with representatives from political bodies and academics. It was the first conference at which police officers from East and West have met in such large numbers. This in itself was a turning point in the history of policing. Since the fall of the Berlin Wall in 1989, cooperation between East and West has increasingly been taking place on different levels.

During the conference, the organising committee developed the idea to edit the lectures given and publish the proceedings, as a number of important arguments and observations were put forward.

In the first place, international policing is a somewhat 'neglected' area of interest. As the world gets 'smaller' due to political, economic, social and technological developments (cyberspace), an evident need arises to understand the implications for (inter)national policing.

In the second place, professionalisation of (inter)national policing must be more than a verbal exchange of ideas in a conference setting. To understand the nature and challenges of international policing, ideas and discussions have to be set down in writing. In this way people who could not attend the conference can form their own opinions and learn from new developments. And because so many intriguing and challenging processes are at work, a publication such as this one can be used to formulate common themes and points of reference.

On a political level we are witnessing growing integration of international police cooperation into international political structures. The Maastricht Treaty laid down the principles for political unification in Europe. Whereas international police cooperation has for decades been a more or less 'private affair' between different police individuals, it is now being drawn into a more formalistic and essentially rule of law context.

International police cooperation is influenced in this way as it is through the activities of different international organisations. The Council of Europe, the United Nations and the European Community are all developing principles guiding the judicial, operational and especially training dimensions of international police cooperation.

Mr. Leuprecht, Deputy Secretary-General to the Council of Europe, draws attention from a historical perspective to the three pillars of (inter)national policing. To him, these are: the fact that it is embedded in democratic structures, that it follows the rule of law and that it respects human rights.

The Dutch Minister of the Interior, Mr. Dijkstal, stresses the need for international treaties and agreements to 'govern' international law enforcement. But the formal aspects, although essential, have to be complemented with the transfer of knowledge between police officials. International police cooperation is about treaties, but is also about 'getting to know one another'. Trust and confidence can be fostered by the exchange of ideas, developments and an open mind towards different cultures and traditions. Conferences such as this are the stage for the transfer of knowledge. The political integration then needs to be supplemented with all sorts of cooperation on an operational and training level. Dijkstal, as Leuprecht, emphasises the need for cooperation especially in the field of training. International police cooperation has become a profession in its own right, and this profession calls for special (new) skills and qualities of police officers. This conference also afforded an excellent opportunity to policing professionals.

Mr. Van Zunderd, from the Rotterdam-Rijnmond police and Vice-President of the IACP, elaborates on the theme of professionalisation. He introduces an international scholarship for senior officers. The subject will be discussed at the June 1997 Board meeting of the IACP. Van Zunderd, as Leuprecht and Dijkstal, regards education and training as vital for international cooperation. Education and training create common references and set international standards. This will enable us to compare developments. The IACP is planning to set up a database to store relevant information on a number of subjects, which will enable police forces around the world to learn from each other's experiences.

The transfer of knowledge has an operational and a political objective. Through education and training, the values and ethics underlying (inter)national policing can be shared. In the eyes of Leuprecht, the philosophical and political roots of policing a democratic society need to be exported (and imported) by countries entering the new democratic world order. Training is an instrument in democracy-building. International police cooperation in this way far exceeds pure instrumental needs in a specific case. For some commentators, policing, that is the preventive, decentralised model, is promoted in the international arena to stimulate the democratic process.

There were contributions by representatives from different countries and institutions; from both the East and the West. Speakers from the USA, Western Europe (Ireland, United Kingdom, France, Italy, the Netherlands) and Eastern Europe (Hungary, Russia) shared their views on crime, law enforcement and cooperation. The multi-disciplinary approach showed itself in the exchange of ideas between police officers from East and West and, as mentioned above, through the contributions from political bodies such as the United Nations and the Council of Europe.

The academic world was also present at the conference. International policing increasingly draws academic researchers into the arena. Lawyers and social scientists, mostly sociologists, criminologists and scholars with an interest in political science contribute at a theoretical and an empirical level to the field of international policing.

Mr. Taylor shares with us his views on some sociological developments in Western society which influence international crime and law enforcement responses. He introduces the somewhat controversial ideas developed by Huntington about 'The Clash of Civilisations'. Essentially, these ideas spring from a well of cultural pessimism. Mr. Leuprecht 'strongly disagrees' with the ideas expressed, which he considers to be 'extremely dangerous'.

Mr. Savona, a leading Italian scholar, draws attention to the increasing intertwining of criminal organisations and financial institutions in money-laundering schemes. On a conceptual level, criminologists face the challenge of analysing, on the one hand, traditional organised crime mostly associated with drugs, prostitution, car theft or protection. On the other hand, white-collar crime, organisational crime or political corruption must be addressed. The term 'white-collar crime' refers to criminal behaviour by respected members of society: public and private managers, employees, organisations, politicians and public officials. Abuse of power, fraud and corruption are a structural feature of legal processes and structures. Is the criminal intelligence process of (inter)national law enforcement adequately structured to analyse these forms of crime? What is the level of crime analysis in international law enforcement? Is it still oriented towards the traditional 'criminal environment' or do we witness changes into areas such as economic crime: environmental crime, fraud with European Community subsidies, tax fraud, insider trading, business espionage or computer crime?

Representatives from all disciplines find themselves around the common theme: the internationalisation of crime.

Mr. Bakker, from the Rotterdam police, speaks about the emerging new economic order in Eastern Europe as a potential risk factor. It fosters crime, both by traditional criminal elements and 'respected' members becoming active in the new money-oriented society exploring the limits of the market place.

Mr. Leuprecht sees 'changes in scenery' and 'new threats and challenges'. He speaks not only of crime in the above-mentioned sense. He also warns us about aggressive nationalism, racism, xenophobia, intolerance and corruption. They too have an impact on policing and on the police themselves. Democratic order and the rule of law can be challenged by these social and political developments.

Mr. Dijkstal points to the growing economic integration within Europe and the accompanying growth of crime. National boundaries have become diffuse. Money, goods and crime have become export products. The interdependencies between societies are complex and demand law enforcement responses.

The organising committee chose two central themes for the conference: community policing and organisational crime. Community policing refers to a combination of structural, functional and ideological ideas underlying policing. The structural – or organisational – principle guiding policing is that of an essentially decentralised police organisation close to and in cooperation with civilians. Community policing addresses the needs of society rather then the needs of the state. The 'team policing' concept is the most outspoken organisational principle of community policing.

The functional idea of community policing basically is the prevention of crime. Community policing is oriented towards the prevention of petty crime, combating feelings of insecurity in local society, and the prevention of small-scale public disorder. The constant and highly visible presence of the police officer in the streets of our cities prevents crime and makes possible an immediate reaction to crime and disturbances.

The ideological idea behind community policing is the improvement of the quality of life through the prevention of crime, together with immediate interaction with civilians if crimes do occur.

Community policing has its philosophical roots in the idea of policing as an essential ingredient of the democratic way of life.

According to Mr. del Buono, Interregional Advisor for Crime Prevention at the United Nations, community policing can only be understood as a new and more democratic paradigm of law enforcement. Community policing is the result of a long institutional, legal, and cultural history very characteristic to Western society. In this way the concept differs dramatically from the militaristic and above all repressive policing in former Eastern societies. This police-model relied heavily on the use of force, torture and a network of informants. State objectives were dominant. The public service orientation, the central feature of community policing, was absent.

Mr. del Buono's analysis of the differences in political culture, and consequently of the dominant police function between East and West, touches upon one of the challenges for the future of policing: the introduction of the democratic model into the emerging new political order in Eastern Europe. He discusses the role of the United Nations in the progress towards community policing through the Crime Prevention Program and the United Nations Development Program. The United Nations is assisting developing countries and countries in transition in shaping their criminal justice systems, reforming constitutional and legal settings, and re-training their criminal justice personnel.

Mr. del Buono's contribution, as that of Mr. Leuprecht, offers a good example of the efforts made by international political bodies towards democratic policing around the world.

Mr. Taylor, professor at the University of York (UK), also addresses community policing. As an academic, being somewhat of an intellectual jester at the court of kings and police commissioners, Mr. Taylor makes the discussion even more complex with his 'broadly pessimistic view of the future'. Essentially, Mr. Taylor's views centre around the growing tensions in society. Community policing addresses the needs of the community, but this community is becoming more and more fragmented. In the light of political violence and international terrorism there are limitations to the contribution of community policing, according to Mr. Taylor. Next, a clear picture is sketched in which Western civilisation will become the theatre of political dissent. These are forces that need to be understood because, according to Mr. Taylor, they effectively relate policing to community aspirations and structures. The ideological premise of community policing – depending on public support – meets with resistance. The effect will be a gradual decline of community policing and the introduction of more repressive elements. Mr. Taylor's views, critiqued by Mr. Leuprecht, draw, as mentioned above, from the well of cultural pessimism. His ideas of the future of policing are in clear contradiction with the historical developments presented by other speakers. Essentially, Mr. Taylor's view is not that the democratic model of policing will be exported to non- Western countries, but that this model will erode in Western societies due to societal developments.

Mr. Frazier, Commissioner of the Baltimore Police, brings us to the heart of community policing in the American city. Mr. Frazier defines community policing in terms of: prevention, the solving of on-going problems and the improvement of the quality of life. He describes the Baltimore Violent Crime and Task Force, a major building block in community policing strategy in great detail. He especially stresses the need to build partnerships with the local community. Law-abiding citizens need to be integrated into community policing initiatives. Part of Mr. Frazier's strategy is the notion of 'regaining territory block by block'. Essentially, this is what community policing is all about. His nine district commanders now have real authority and real responsibility for their individual districts. They are in charge of directing their resources in their districts strategically, identifying strong blocks and extending the strengths found there to 'convert' adjacent blocks. In particular, the commanders and officers must draw upon the resources of caring, active individuals within the community.

On an informal basis, concerned citizens influence their fellow neighbours to keep up their homes, alleys and streets, as well as cooperating with police to prevent and solve crimes. This year, the efforts of these individuals will be supported and others will be recruited into service through a pro-active Block Representative Program. Community leaders will be worked with to stimulate interest in the programme and conduct training.

Mr. Hessing, Chief Constable of the Rotterdam-Rijnmond Police, gives an historical overview of community policing in the Netherlands. The bureaucratic organisational structure of the late sixties led to inefficiencies. The primary work process was separated, compartmentalised and drew heavily on hierarchy and authority. Community policing was introduced as a new ideological and organisational concept. Activities of the police should not only be guided by repressive objectives. Instead, an orientation towards prevention and the local needs of civilians came to the fore. This ideological change led to organisational changes. Centralisation was replaced by decentralisation, and compartmentalisation made way for the integration of specialised police tasks into small units working near the public. The police now are concerned with a wide variety of activities, ranging from rendering assistance in emergencies, advising, corrective action, repression, supervision and detection. In addition, the police contribute to the implementation of local arrangements in which they stimulate local authorities, social institutions and the public to develop their own prevention strategies. Mr. Hessing introduces the policing paradox. On the one hand, government should promote security or even guarantee it by taking action itself. On the other hand, government should promote public and social institutions to take preventive action itself and remain passive. As a government body, the police is trapped in this paradox. According to Mr. Hessing, only the empowerment of other parties rather than increasing police power is the solution to this dilemma. Community policing essentially strives for synthesis between police professionalisation and the external orientation in applying it. Next, Mr. Hessing gives an overview of community policing in Rotterdam. Both the Baltimore and Rotterdam experiences in community policing give the reader a broad overview of this police model in daily practice.

Mr. Sutka, Chief of Police of Hadjú Bihar, Hungary, places community policing in the political turmoil of a society undergoing fundamental political, economic and social changes. The police were unprepared as regards both structure and working methods for these radical changes. The state-oriented, centralised and repressive police model needed to be adjusted to the demands of the new era. The relationship with the public, traditionally a hostile one, had to improve. More time was to be invested in improving public security, and the executive policeman had to develop a new attitude.

Along with political changes, the police were faced with a sharply increasing rise in the level of crime. The removal of the shackles of the old regime caused a widespread crime problem that even endangered social reform. The Hungarian police adopted a new police structure inspired by ideological and organisational principles of Western community policing. The essence was an expedient re-grouping of existing staff and technical implements aimed at integrating various service branches – public security, crime – into one organisation. This was accompanied by decentralisation, both of lines of command and organisational units. This made it possible to work close to the public, and to introduce the concept of accountability for local units. Along with these changes, a re-orientation towards prevention and a public service orientation took place.

The second theme of the conference was *organised crime* and *organisational crime*. In many of the contributions, organised crime refers to traditional criminal organisations, like the Italian Mafia, with one principal goal: to supply illegal products to illegal markets. Illegal products predominately associated with organised crime, of course, are drugs. Other 'products' mentioned are protection, extortion and prostitution. Illegal markets have always been the main target of organised crime. The scene however is shifting; so is the nature of criminal organisations.

Mr. Savona's contribution right at the start of the second day made this clear. Mr. Savona pointed at the thin line between illegal and legal markets. The latter are infiltrated by organised crime groups seeking new, illegal profits. But the concept of infiltration does not fully cover the definition of crime in our societies. The business community itself, faced with increasing competition, combines legal activities with illegal activities. From a criminological perspective, this is referred to as white-collar crime, business crime or organisational crime. These activities are conducted by respected members of society working for legitimate enterprises: financial institutions, accountancy firms, trading companies, lawyers and production companies. Sometimes this is being done for individual profit. Sometimes for the benefit of the net profit of the organisation.

As was the case with the first topic, a distinguished list of speakers shared their views. The multinational and multi-disciplinary character was prevalent in dealing with organised crime and organisational crime in such different countries as Italy, Germany, France, the United Kingdom, the United States and Russia.

Mr. Savona gave examples of business crimes: fraud against the European Union, fraud in the building sector and the waste-disposal sector. Sometimes the business community is used as a front for organised crime. Sometimes the business community initiates the fraud itself. Especially in the area of money-laundering, illegal and legal markets meet in the offices of financial institutions. In the Italian case the lines between underworld and 'upperworld' have become more diffuse through the involvement of political parties, not only in shady dealings with the Mafia but also in 'assisting' business crime. Markets in which the lines are blurred are the product market, the labour market and the capital market (including the stock market). Mr. Savona introduces the concept of collusive agreements to describe the dynamic nature of crime and the ever-changing nature of cooperation between criminal and legal players in the criminal arena.

This new complexity is also described by Mr. Maass, representing the Bundeskriminalambt. No clearly definable legal element, mostly constituted of individual offences, can describe organised crime. Mr. Maass, like all of us, is faced with a rather complex phenomenon. Since 1991, the

German government publishes annual reports on organised crime. He discusses some of the recent findings. Apart from traditional examples of organised crime (illegal markets, the use of violence, bribery, extortion and corruption), Mr. Maass also talks about the exploitation of commercial structures. In 1995, commercial structures were exploited with regard to half the investigations analysed. Financial investigations are to become an even more central ingredient of the criminal investigation process because of this combination of legal and illegal activities. This is especially so with regard to money-laundering.

From Germany we then move away from the continent and enter the United Kingdom. Mr. Veness, New Scotland Yard, discusses serious crime threats. The first part of the chapter is devoted to yet another problem in law enforcement: terrorism. This is discussed with respect to its best-known perpetrator, the IRA, but animal extremism, environmental extremism and religious movements are also mentioned. Still, the major threat to the UK is overwhelmingly the enormous amount of local crime. Mr. Veness looks into the future of policing, and presents us with some essential elements: it must be multi-disciplinary, multi-agency and above all multinational. Like other speakers, Mr. Veness also stresses the need to have financial investigations integrated into the criminal investigative process.

Mr. Ringgold, Deputy Director of the FBI, provides an insight into the American experience with organised crime. The 'melting pot' characteristic of the United States, something in which Americans take great pride, has a by-product: virtually every known organised criminal group operating in the world has its representatives in the USA. Traditionally, Italian criminal groups operate in this country. Mr. Ringgold gives an historical overview of different groups. But the palette of criminal organisations is more colourful. Asian, Nigerian and Eurasian groups are also active. In 1992, the FBI initiated its major focus on Eurasian crime, in particular on crime related to the immigrant population from the former Soviet Union. Among the 200,000 or so immigrants, the FBI estimates that there were about 2,000 criminals. At least 25 formal Eurasian gangs have been identified. Mr Ringgold discusses the FBI approach since 1992. The traditional police techniques proved to have a limited impact. The FBI realised the need for international police cooperation. This led to an intensive effort to work together with law enforcement agencies in different east Europe states. The FBI established an office in Moscow, and has set up a programme introducing ideas and methods to the Eurasian countries. Law enforcement officials from these countries travel to major cities in the USA and assist in surveillance, interpretation of wire-taps and case preparation. In addition the FBI invites officers to the Police Academy at Quantico. The FBI also initiated a cooperative venture in Hungary. This led among other things to the establishment of the International Law Enforcement Academy in Budapest.

Mr. Peduzzi and Mr. Guimezanes bring us back to the origins of modern policing in the early 19th century. In the aftermath of the French revolution the state created a law enforcement apparatus. One of the first leading officials was François Vidocq, an adventurer and ex-convict. He became head of the Sûreté, a department which itself was staffed by ex-prisoners. The fight against crime – and especially white-collar crime – undoubtedly requires an intimate knowledge of the circles in which criminals operate. This was true in the days of Vidocq, and still forms the key element of criminal analysis and investigations, although the recruitment techniques seem to have undergone some changes since then.

Mr. Peduzzi and Mr. Guimezanes give an insight into the functioning of the judicial police in France. The training component is viewed as a vital element of law enforcement. Interestingly, the French Judicial Police have given priority to economic and financial training (money-laundering, law on property, stock exchange, computer fraud and the futures market). This seems to be a common theme. As is the case in Germany, the educational process in the United Kingdom and, for instance Italy, is gradually moving towards different forms of financial investigations. The use of data-processing within the French police has undergone rapid changes. This is an essential basis for investigating criminal or financial matters.

Mr. Peduzzi and Mr. Guimezanes also stress the need for international cooperation. Law enforcement officials work as liaisons abroad and some agencies, such as the Central Office for the Repression of Drug-trafficking, have set up offices in foreign countries.

Mr. Petrov, Deputy Minister of the Interior of the Russian Federation, discusses the crime situation and emerging trends in Russia. The political and accompanying economic and social changes after the fall of the Berlin Wall led to a rapidly rising crime problem. Mr. Petrov points to some positive developments. A number of crime statistics indicate a decrease. However, illegal drug-trafficking has become a serious problem. So has economic crime and, although some successes have been achieved, it poses a serious threat to Russian society. Misappropriation of state property in the course of privatisation and abuse in its administration, together with illegal redistribution of state capital, was a main feature of criminality in 1995. The market forces stimulated selfish motivations in private business and led, for instance, to large-scale fraud to the detriment of investors by various financial institutions. Next Mr. Petrov looks into the future of policing. It is worth noting that the main trends and developments in the crime situation are not likely to change significantly. Changes in the economic, political and social spheres are likely to influence the criminal situation continuously. 1996 will most probably be marked by an aggravated competition for property, characterised by armed clashes and the violent seizures or destruction of assets. The clash of selfish interests with the beginning of a new stage of revision of zones of influence between criminal structures, together with criminal penetration into the sphere of the most profitable projects of the economy, can become a powerful catalyst in the worsening of the criminal situation in the country.

Shadow businesses in the credit and financial sphere, and in investment charity funds, are likely to expand. There will be a rise in the number of fraud schemes with bank guarantees, credit cards, financial embezzlement at banks by means of computer-related crime. A spreading of the influence of organised crime, not only within CIS countries but also as regards other countries, as well as an increase in laundering of criminal assets abroad can be expected. International criminal economic and multi-purpose structures will be more active in the spheres of the illegal export of precious and non-ferrous metals and other raw materials.

Finally, Mr. Pintèr, Commissioner of the Hungarian National Police, analyses conditions facilitating international and organisational crime from the perspective both of the perpetrators and law enforcement. Mr. Pintèr's chapter draws together a number of themes and developments from the different participants. From the perspective of the perpetrators, Mr. Pintèr points to the freedom of movement, the establishment of cross-national personal contacts, the opportunity to escape prosecution by resettling in other countries, the almost baffling mushrooming of international business enterprises and the investment of laundering of criminal money in other countries. The future of crime lies in internationalisation. From the perspective of law enforcement, Mr. Pintèr indicates hurdles on the road to a truly international, multi-agency approach. There are different degrees of readiness to cooperate; we lack adequate knowledge of each other's legal systems, organisational structures and operational procedures. This is further influenced by problems of communication and the lack of a uniformity of terms. Next there are obstacles put up by data protection, the differences in the current level of training and the differences between national documents issued for the same purpose. These are but a few problems that need to be addressed, according to Mr. Pintèr.

This realistic analysis is followed by an exposé of factors facilitating international cooperation: defining common goals, achieving similarity of principles of methodology and criminal tactics and, among other things, up-to-date police officer training. Mr. Pintèr explains the origins and functioning of the Central European Police Academy, which has become a forum of further training where police officers can deepen their knowledge and share their experiences in combating organised crime. Topics dealt with are terrorism, illegal drug-trafficking, illegal gun-running, organisational crime, and also economic and environmental crime.

Mr. Pintèr also discusses the International Law Enforcement Academy. He foresees the three levels of education in the following arrangement: the first would admit colleagues with a high level of theoretical and practical knowledge, who, after an analysis of international experience, would discuss concepts of scientific-academic value, and would adopt them for purposes of future cooperation. On the second level, mainly middle and top-level executives from criminal investigation and public safety speciality fields would come together. They would be given assistance primarily with respect to their short-term planning and in executing their day-to-day tasks. The third level would involve basically crime officers, but also public safety officers interfacing with the citizens on a daily basis, *i.e.* uniformed street police officers that would come together. This form of further training may seem unrealistic today, because the conditions for it in fact do not yet exist. A citizen of a Europe to be unified in the future, however, has every right to expect to feel – and be – safe. No matter which country he goes to on the continent, he expects to be able to turn with confidence to an officer of the national police, and he expects the procedures of the authorities to be very much of the same standard as those in his own country.

Finally, we would like to express our gratitude to our partners in the organisation of the conference:

- the Hadjú Bihar Police, Debrecen, Hungary

- the Baltimore Police Department, Maryland, USA

- the European Law Enforcement College (ELEC)

- the Erasmus Centre for Police Studies (ECPS) of the Erasmus University in Rotterdam.

ABOUT THE AUTHORS

Kees Bakker (The Netherlands)

Kees Bakker started his career with the Rotterdam police in 1967. He held a number of positions before he became Chief Constable of the Ridderkerk police in 1981. He returned to the Rotterdam-Rijnmond police as a member of the force's management. In this capacity he led operation 'Victor', a campaign to fight drugs. He represents the Netherlands in the 'strategic committee' with France to fight drugs. He is a member of the International Policy Committee of the International Association of Chiefs of Police.

Hans Dijkstal (The Netherlands)

Hans Dijkstal was appointed Deputy Prime Minister and Minister of the Interior in the Kok Government in August 1994. He was a Member of Parliament from 1982 to 1994.

Peter van Zunderd (The Netherlands)

Peter van Zunderd started his career with the police in 1963 as a sailor with the Rotterdam River police. After graduating from the Dutch Police Academy, he became police inspector in 1978. He held a number of positions in the Rotterdam police force before he became Chief Constable of the Capelle aan den IJssel police in 1988. In 1992 he was promoted to district manager in the Groot-IJsselmonde area (which also features the Feijenoord football stadium). In 1995 he was appointed International Vice President of the International Association of the Chiefs of Police.

Peter Leuprecht (Council of Europe, France)

Peter Leuprecht gained a law degree in 1959 at the University of Innsbruck (Austria). Until 1961 he worked as an assistant at this university in the Institute of Public Law. From 1961 until 1972 he held several positions in different departments of the Parliamentary Assembly; from 1972 until 1976 he served as Head of Division in the Office of the Clerk, until 1980 as Secretary of the Committee of Ministers and till 1993 as Director of Human Rights. Since 1993, he has held the position of Deputy Secretary-General of the Council of Europe in Strasbourg, France.

Vincent del Buono (United Nations, Austria)

Vincent del Buono serves at the Crime Prevention and Criminal Justice Division of the United Nations. He is currently posted in Vienna, Austria.

Professor Max Taylor (Ireland)

Max Taylor has written and lectured around the world on security issues, especially as regards terrorism and organised crime. He has organised and run a number of humanitarian aid projects in various war-torn areas of the world. He is a member of the Executive Board of Europe 2000 and the Advisory Board of ELEC. He works at the University of York in the Irish Republic.

Thomas C. Frazier (USA)

He started his career as a police officer in 1967. He served in the San José Police Department in several fields as officer, Sergeant, Lieutenant, Captain and Deputy Chief before he was appointed in 1994 as Police Commissioner in Baltimore (US). He participates in several organisations in Baltimore, such as the Fraternal Order of Police and the Vanguard Justice Society, and he is Chairman of the Governor's Community Oriented Policing and Juvenile Justice Subcommittees.

Rob Hessing (The Netherlands)

He started his career with the Municipal Police in Hilversum (the Netherlands). In 1982, after having been stationed in Apeldoorn and Oss he was appointed Chief of Police in Eindhoven. In 1989 he was appointed Chief of Police in Rotterdam and subsequently in 1992 became Chief of Police for the whole Rotterdam-Rijnmond area. He is Chairman for police activities on environmental issues and President of the European Association of Air- and Seaport Police, and is a member of the Board of the International Association of Air- and Seaport Police.

Sandor Sutka (Hungary)

He graduated from the Police Academy in 1979 as a crime investigator. His first job was to work as a uniformed policeman in Békéscsaba (Hungary). In 1986, he became Head of the Town Police of Békéscsaba. He meanwhile finished Law School and gained his law degree. In 1990 he became the Chief Commander of Hadjú Bihar County Police in Debrecen.

Professor Ernesto U. Savona (Italy)

Ernesto Savona has a law degree from Palermo University and followed postgraduate studies at the University of Rome. He is President of the European Documentation and Research Network on cross-border crime, a foundation promoted by the European Commission and grouping sixteen European Universities. He is consultant to the United Nations Crime Program, the Council of Europe and various national governments and Scientific Advisor to ISPAC. He has published several papers and books focusing on the relationships between organisational crime and criminal justice systems.

He holds a position as Professor of Criminology and Director of Transcrime at the Faculty of Law, Trento University.

Harald Maass (Germany)

Since 1977 Harald Maass has been senior officer at the Bundeskriminalamt, where he is in charge of: international police cooperation, investigation of organisational crime, organised crime intelligence. He is also seconded to ICPO-GS (Head of European Secretariat)

David Veness (United Kingdom)

David Veness entered the Metropolitan Cadet Corps in 1964 and became a CID officer in 1969. He held various positions in North, East and Central London as a detective, and in different specialist capacities. He was appointed Commander in 1987 and served with Royalty and Diplomatic Protection until 1990. In 1990 he became Commander Public Order, Territorial Security and Operational Support. He was promoted to Deputy Assistant Commissioner 'Specialist Operations' Crime in 1991 in Scotland. He is Secretary of the Chief Officers Committee of the South East Regional Crime Squad. He currently holds the position of Appointed Assistant Commissioner in charge of all Specialist Operations, which include protection, terrorism, security and organised crime.

Alan G. Ringgold (USA)

Alan Ringgold joined the FBI in 1970 and became a specialist in Italian organised crime. In 1978 he started managing labour racketeering investigations in Boston, Massachusetts. From 1980 until 1982 he served at FBI Headquarters in the Organised Crime Section, where he initiated the relationships between the FBI and the Italian police services. In 1982 he was transferred to Bern as the Assistant Legal Attaché and promoted to Legal Attaché in 1985 with responsibility for liaison activities in Switzerland, Austria and Liechtenstein. In 1987 he was designated exchange manager with the Drug Enforcement Agency in Washington, and in 1989 he was appointed Legal Attaché in Paris, from which position he managed FBI liaison with France and half the African continent. In 1994 he was promoted to the rank of Inspector and appointed as Deputy Assistant Director.

Jacques Guimezanes (France)

Jacques Guimezanes has a master's degree in Private Law. He became a Superintendent in charge of investigations on white-collar crime. In 1982 he was appointed Chief Superintendent, head of the management of staff and logistics of the National Crime Investigation Department. He became Commander, head of the service seconded to the economic and financial investigations in 1994, and was promoted to Deputy National Director. In January 1996 he was promoted to Deputy National Director for crime, in charge of economic and financial investigations

Valery Petrov (Russian Federation)

Valery Petrov is Lieutenant General of Militia, First Deputy Minister of the Interior and Head of the Organised Crime Control Department.

Sandor Pintèr (Hungary)

Mr. Pintèr completed studies at the police high school, the University of Law, and entered the district police of Budapest in 1972. In 1985 he became Vice-Commandant in a commissariat, and in 1990 Vice-Commandant in the Pest County police force. In 1991 he was appointed as Chief of Police of Budapest and Chief of the National Police.

Dr. Bob Hoogenboom (The Netherlands)

Bob Hoogenboom is Director of the Erasmus Centre for Police Studies (ECPS) at the Erasmus University in Rotterdam. He teaches at the Dutch National Police Academy. He has published on the history of policing, regulatory agencies, private policing, private investigations and political and criminal intelligence. The ECPS conducts research into policing, organised crime, fraud, money-laundering and the privatisation of policing.

Max Meiboom (The Netherlands)

Max Meiboom joined the Rotterdam-Rijnmond Regional Police in 1994. He studied English Language and Literature at Leiden University. He was Deputy Mayor of Capelle aan den IJssel from 1986 until 1994. He currently holds a position as policy advisor with the Regional Criminal Investigation Unit.

Dick Schoneveld (The Netherlands)

He holds the rank of Commissioner. He currently heads the International Relations Project.

Hans Stoop (The Netherlands)

He joined the police in 1966. He holds the rank of Police Inspector. He currently works in the Public Relations Department of the Rotterdam-Rijnmond Regional Police.

1. IACP AND CONFERENCE THEMES

C.K. Bakker

1. East meets West

Rotterdam is not just the driving force of the Dutch economy; it is above all the gateway to Europe. As the world's largest port, Rotterdam occupies a special position between Europe on one hand, and America and Asia on the other hand. Due to its international contacts, Rotterdam is pre-eminently in a position to form a bridge between East and West, between the old and the new world. But also, because of its geographical position on the European continent, Rotterdam may be expected to be a bridge between the countries of Western Europe and those of Central and Eastern Europe. Our international position compels us to look far beyond our own borders, and that is why we are pleased to host this conference.

The assistance we were given by our sister forces, the Baltimore City Police Department from the United States of America and the Hajdú Bihar Police from Debrecen, Hungary, once more stresses the fact that this conference is the venue where East and West meet.

2. A secure Europe

A secure Europe, at least a Europe that is as secure as possible, is in everyone's interest. The positive development of the new relationship between the West European and the East European countries, and the new social structure in the East European countries, unfortunately, also give cause for concern. One of the most striking and alarming developments is the growth of organised crime. In virtually no time, criminal organisations have acquired economically strong positions and they prove to have such large funds available that they can hardly be stopped from penetrating both the West European under- and business world. One of the factors weakening our combative force is the new economic order in Central and Eastern Europe. Frequently these countries lack the self-regulating mechanisms and checking possibilities that give Western countries an immense advantage. As an example, I could mention the management of and the checks on the banking- and accountancy sectors. The open borders of the new Europe make it easier than ever before to export crime and set up large-scale networks.

Some years ago, the then Minister of the Interior of the Netherlands, Ien Dales, initiated a special form of cooperation between the police in the Netherlands and the police in Hungary. This initiative was meant not only to serve mutual interests; the basic principle was the moral duty felt in the Netherlands to support the young democracies in building up a modern constitutional state. A large number of Dutch police forces responded to this appeal, and have in the meantime realised some form of cooperation with the Hungarian police force. Through this special cooperation we wish to make our know-how and experience available to another European country. Welcoming know-how and experience gained in other countries first of all demands personal contacts and trust. We all know that these have to grow, and cannot be forced or imposed on anyone. This conference is an excellent forum at which to establish contacts and mutually to open doors. We have therefore made special efforts to invite to Rotterdam as many representatives as possible from police forces in Central and Eastern Europe. To realise this we have introduced an adoption system, by which police forces in Western countries have made financial contributions to enable their colleagues from Central and Eastern Europe to attend this international and intercontinental conference. I am pleased that many forces in the Netherlands have supported this initiative. In addition, a significant contribution has been made by the United States. I would particularly like to mention the Federal Law Enforcement Agency and the IACP itself. I would also like to draw attention to the fact that the Dutch government has supported us in every respect in organising this conference. The Minister of the Interior has shown his particular interest in this conference by at present being in our midst and opening this conference officially, but also in supporting its organisation, both financially and by making staff available. We owe our gratitude to the Mayor and Council of Rotterdam. Furthermore, I should point out that the Ministry of Foreign Affairs has granted a substantial subsidy enabling the Dutch police forces to allow Central and Eastern European colleagues to attend this conference.

3. Globalising police cooperation

Today we are very proud to do so. We welcome 45 participants from eleven Central and East European countries. I think that this large participation by representatives of police forces from Central and Eastern Europe is highly significant. My hopes are that this system of adoption, which essentially consists of a sponsoring initiative, will be followed by the organisers of future conferences. Apart from the growing bilateral contacts between the West European police and the police in Central and Eastern Europe, we have also given a great deal of prominence to the interest from the United States in the police in Europe. This is demonstrated in the first place by the major participation in this conference by our colleagues from the United States. I view the large delegation from the Board of Officers of the IACP as a sign of growing awareness of the importance of globalising police cooperation. We shall have plenty of opportunity to revitalise and expand existing contacts. In addition I would also like to revert to an American initiative that is of particular interest for Europe. Some time ago, the United States Federal Police Agencies initiated the foundation of a European Law Enforcement Academy in Budapest, Hungary. At this Academy, a wide variety of experts and coaches from the United States teach in courses for interested police forces from Central and Eastern Europe. On several occasions our friends from the United States have invited the West European Police Services to participate in this initiative. It has been suggested several times to have the work of the Academy in Budapest supported by Western European countries as well, not only financially but also materially, by delegating teachers and experts. International police cooperation is more than just exchanging expertise or clarifying norms and values. It is equally important, to say the least, to translate these into legal systems, a process which requires respect for historical, cultural and social aspects. Given the diversity of these aspects in our European society, I hope that this conference will contribute to the West European countries accepting the invitation from the United States to join the Budapest Academy.

2. TRANSFER OF KNOWLEDGE: THE KEY PRINCIPLE

H.F. Dijkstal

1. The need for international cooperation

Although we tend to associate the concept of international cooperation with treaties and agreements on which cooperation is based, in practice cooperation usually begins by getting to know one another. By this I mean that we must have confidence in one another, and show an open-minded interest in each other's culture, traditions and developments. As we say in the Netherlands, we must 'know and be known', a phrase that should apply not only to relations between the police and the public, but to international relations as well.

It is now an established fact that the police need to look, and indeed are looking, beyond their national borders if they are to tackle contemporary problems – problems which I am sure do not need to be enumerated here. In the past, occasional meetings were largely organised as pleasant social gatherings, but nowadays the strengthening of personal contacts is an absolute necessity.

International cooperation between police forces has, slowly but surely, become a profession in its own right, and the practice of any profession calls for special skills. This new task not only puts a demand on existing police knowledge and police skills, but it also demands new qualities in police officers. Knowledge of languages is but one example. The importance of discussing this matter in an international setting should not be underestimated, and I think that this conference affords an excellent opportunity.

2. The importance of Central and Eastern Europe

The fall of the Berlin Wall in 1989 has had a tremendous impact on the contacts between East and West. It has made East and West European societies accessible to one another. This development is reflected not only in the economic sector, with economic relations becoming increasingly inter-dependent, but also in the field of crime, where the same problems now affect both Western and Eastern Europe alike. These include forms of organised crime such as traffic in women, traffic in stolen cars and, above all, the drugs problem. There is no doubt that both East and West stand to benefit from close cooperation in tackling these problems.

A clearer picture of the types of crime and their extent, in other people's countries, is necessary. Knowledge and techniques therefore need to be exchanged. This transfer of knowledge should also have a significant democratic dimension. A police force which is oriented towards the public, which forms an integral part of a democratic-constitutional state, and which looks to the future, is in keeping with a democratic Europe in which the East-West frontiers have been dismantled.

The enlargement of the European Union is an important theme at the Intergovernmental Conference. It will have a major influence, especially on decision-making within the European Union. From the standpoint of police cooperation and security, the accession of Central and Eastern European countries to the Union is a logical following step, but such a large number of countries makes it more difficult to reach decisions. The decision-making structure, therefore, will have to be changed. One possible solution for this problem will be the multi-speed concept.

3. Community policing and organised crime

The themes selected for this conference deal with two vital aspects of police work: community policing and tackling organised crime. The first is aimed at ensuring the closest possible contact with the public, whilst the other involves a very difficult task for the police and judicial authorities.

It is very important to support the efforts being made in these fields in Central and Eastern Europe. The Netherlands is devoting a great deal of attention to this. It is in itself a good thing that our countries already maintain intensive bilateral contacts, but, given the international dimension of crime, cooperation with Central and Eastern European countries needs to be coordinated more vigorously in the European Union than it has been hitherto.

In the context of the European Union too, it is therefore important to transfer as much knowledge and expertise as possible to Central and Eastern European countries, and to ensure that support for Central and Eastern European countries is better coordinated and streamlined. The Council of Europe and the European Union already invest a lot of effort in this task.

Cooperation between East and West must remain an important topic of discussion in the European context, and I shall therefore do everything in my power to encourage the developments that are already in progress.

4. Conclusion

As you all know, and as our widespread trade-relationships also show, the international orientation of the Netherlands has a long tradition. I am pleased that this outward-looking approach is now to be given shape at a political level too. I am therefore very much interested in the outcome of this East-West conference.

Finally, I would like to congratulate Mr. David Walchek, the President of the IACP, on the choice of topics, the large turnout and, last but not least, for choosing Rotterdam as the venue. This city has always been a centre of international trade, and now has the honour of hosting this international conference.

3. SETTING STANDARDS: TRAINING IS ESSENTIAL

P.J. van Zunderd

1. Introduction

When the International Association of Chiefs of Police (IACP) was founded more than a century ago, the world was a different place. It was much simpler in so many ways. What was happening in Europe in those days was of little importance to other regions in the world, and vice versa. But today, almost all of a sudden, the world has grown smaller. Computers, fax machines and satellite communications systems reduce to a matter of minutes what used to require days or weeks to accomplish. International business alliances operate as if the principals are across town from one another and, not surprisingly, organised crime has gone global as well: terrorism, drug-trafficking, environmental crime, trade in endangered species, traffic in illegal aliens, money-laundering, etc.

In a world where international crime knows no borders, those of us charged with upholding the law must find ways to cooperate with each other just as criminals have found ways to help each other to break the law. No organisation is in a better position to accomplish this than the IACP. The truly international Association of Chiefs of Police can be of immeasurable benefit to develop standards in countries around the world, especially in new democracies where policing requires measures very different from those that were used under totalitarian regimes. To restore democracy, the civilian police has shown professionalism in various theatres of the United Nations' peace-keeping operations. The police has helped to sow the seed of democracy in Cambodia, Mozambique, Somalia, Haiti, and is engaged in restoring democracy in the Balkan region right now. The involvement of the civilian police in UN missions is one of the many changes in our profession today and is, as such, a very positive change indeed.

2. International scholarship for senior officers

The IACP wants to be a truly global organisation and, in underlining this aim, a proposal will be made for a new international scholarship for senior officers; this proposal will be on the agenda of the Board meeting in June of this year. The principle of this international scholarship is that the enhancement of police professionalism is hardly possible without the addition of a global dimension. On one hand this follows from the fact that many forms of crime use the world as their playground, on the other hand the IACP wants to establish a world-wide search for methods to optimise police work. In spite of – or thanks to – cultural differences, we can learn from each other. Seen in this light, learning in the widest possible context from experiences and working situations elsewhere in the world is a meaningful exercise. The IACP will choose a research theme for a two-year period. I suggest that the first theme for 1997 and 1998 will be community policing. These studies are to be carried out under a standard set-up, so the possibility of comparing the findings will increase. The outcome of the studies will be stored in a database managed at IACP headquarters. Members who wish to orient themselves in the relevant subject will have access to this database. Every two years a renowned scientist will be asked by the IACP to study the data, in order to derive more general conclusions from it, and to publish the results in our monthly magazine, *The Police Chief,* and other leading police journals. Each year a maximum of ten people will receive a scholarship, and every year the IACP will present the results of this programme at the annual conference.

3. The themes of the conference: community policing and organised crime

The topics of this European conference have been carefully chosen. One of the topics is oriented towards trends in community policing. We are all familiar with the old saying that one ounce of prevention is better than a pound of cure. Pro-active policing is a part of the mechanism of preventive action and can be seen as an investment in the future. Today, the majority of the police organisations have adopted this strategy. It is a strategy through which police and citizens work together as partners to improve the quality of life.

The other topic is aimed at discovering trends in organisational crime and, here too, close cooperation between law enforcement agencies in a global perspective is more necessary than ever before. The high standard of professionalism present here will guarantee excellent lectures and discussions. I invite you all to contribute to these discussions so that we can learn from each other, break down borders and build new relations to improve the profession of law enforcement in a global perspective.

4. THE COUNCIL OF EUROPE: DEMOCRACY, RULE OF LAW AND HUMAN RIGHTS

P. Leuprecht

1. Introduction

The Council of Europe is the oldest and largest among the institutions working for closer European unity. It was founded in 1949, one of its principal founding fathers being Sir Winston Churchill. In the beginning it consisted of ten West European countries. Now it has 39 member states, fifteen of which were not so long ago part of the so-called Eastern block, and several of them were Republics of the Soviet Union at the time, such as Russia and the Ukraine. The Council of Europe is in the process of becoming a truly pan-European organisation now. It has also acquired a new dimension as the United States of America has recently obtained an observer status within the Council of Europe. In the meantime Japan and Canada have applied for the same status.

2. Pluralist democracy, rule of law and human rights

Notwithstanding these spectacular changes, it is important to recall the philosophical and political roots of the Council of Europe. These roots go back into the Second World War, into the resistance and fight against Marxism, fascism and totalitarianism. 'Never again' was the motto of the founding fathers. The horrors that had happened, the systematic and massive violations of human rights and human dignity that had been committed, should never be allowed to happen again; they should be prevented by a new European order of peace, built on a collective guarantee of pluralist democracy, rule of law, and human rights. These three concepts, pluralist democracy, rule of law and human rights, are the basic principles of the Council of Europe, laid down in its founding treaty, *The Statutes*, signed in 1949. Respect for the three principles is, at the same time, the main criterion for the admission of a country to the Council of Europe, and is a permanent obligation for all its members. The Council of Europe has set up what is generally recognised as the most advanced international system for the protection and promotion of human rights. In this respect, three of the most important human rights treaties, elaborated and operated by the Council of Europe, can be mentioned here: *The European Convention on Human Rights*, which was signed in 1950, has set up a unique supranational control machinery with the European Commission and the European Court of Human Rights, the judgments of which are legally binding upon member states and have a growing impact on the legal and social reality in our member states; *The European Social Charter*, signed in 1961, which guarantees basic social rights; and the more recent *European Convention for the Prevention of Torture and Inhuman or Degrading Treatment or Punishment.* This convention has introduced entirely new features into international human rights protection by setting up a system of visits or inspections to places where people are deprived of their liberty, as a means of preventing particularly serious violations of human rights, namely torture and inhuman or degrading treatment.

3. Changes of scenery

As a result of the critical and positive changes which have occurred in Europe since 1989, not only the geographical extension, but also the role and mission of the Council of Europe have changed. It was conceived as an organisation for the defence and preservation of pluralist democracy, the rule of law, and human rights. For a long time it had to remain geographically limited, as neither the communist countries in Central and Eastern Europe nor Spain and Portugal under their dictatorships qualified for membership. The pan-European Council of Europe today is increasingly becoming an instrument of democracy-building. It assists the countries of Central and Eastern Europe in developing democratic regimes based on the rule of law and respect for human rights. For this purpose it runs important programmes of cooperation and assistance, some of them in cooperation with the European Union. The main aim of the Council of Europe today is to establish in the greater Europe what the Vienna summit of our heads of state and government in October 1993 called 'democratic security'. Of course, the rapid enlargement of the Council of Europe in the last few years has not taken place without problems. One of the key questions is and will be how the Council in its new composition can maintain its high standards regarding pluralist democracy, the rule of law and human rights. Monitoring the compliance of member states with these commitments is of the utmost importance. It is an absolute necessity if the

Council of Europe is to maintain its effectiveness and credibility, or to put it differently: if it is not to loose its soul.

4. New threats and challenges

Europe, and the causes which the Council of Europe are defending and promoting, are confronted nowadays with serious threats and challenges. Let me mention just a few:

* aggressive nationalism

* ethnocentrism

* racism

* anti-Semitism

* xenophobia and intolerance

* religious fanaticism

* organised crime

* corruption

They all seriously threaten democracy, the rule of law and human rights. Human rights have to be ascertained and defended against any kind of power, not just state power, but any kind of power, be it political, economic or social. Of course, human rights must also be defended against the power of organised crime. Human rights are threatened not only by exorbitant uncontrolled state power, but also by the absence of state power, by a weak deficient state. The mission and duty of a democratic state based on the rule of law is to respect, protect and promote human rights. It must ensure effective respect for human rights. It must be in a position to defend human rights against forces in society that may threaten, undermine and violate these rights.

5. The role of the police in a democratic state

This brings me naturally to the police and its role in a democratic state and a democratic society, which is one of the central concepts of the *European Convention of Human Rights*. It is of course utterly simplistic and stupid to consider the police as a kind of natural or born enemy of human rights. As human beings and most human endeavours, the police are capable of

15

P. Leuprecht

the best and the worst. Just like the state and state power, the police and police power can be protectors but also gravediggers of human rights. It is in my view essential to be absolutely honest when dealing with these issues for which there is no easy answer. If we are honest, we have to recognise that there can of course be a tension between respect for human rights and the exigencies of law enforcement. There is tension between order and liberty; not only at the level of philosophical and moral debate, but also in the daily conduct of our lives. There is no point in denying the existence of this tension and potential conflict. A society without conflict is a fiction of totalitarian regimes. As far as the police are concerned, in a democratic state based on the rule of law, order and liberty have to be reconciled in law and by law. The police are law enforcement officials, which means that they have a duty to respect and enforce human rights, and the laws that protect these human rights. They are certainly not entitled to violate the fundamental laws of human rights when enforcing other laws, or under the pretext of enforcing other laws. If we are honest, we must also recognise that the police are much more exposed to certain risks than others are. They run a far greater risk of being confronted with situations in which human rights might be violated, much greater risks than those active in other professions. In this respect the findings of the European Committee for the Prevention of Torture are revealing and often worrying. This even applies to countries that form part of the Council of Europe. There is obviously a risk, and in many cases more than a risk, of human rights violations occurring, for example when people are arrested by the police, when they are held in police custody, and when they are interrogated by the police. In one of the annual reports of the European Committee for the Prevention of Torture is said the following: *'there is no better guarantee against the ill treatment of a person deprived of his liberty, than a properly trained police officer'* and, personally, I would add to this: a carefully selected and recruited police officer.

6. Police training and human rights

Police training in a democratic society that is based on the rule of law must include human rights education, in order to foster an awareness of human rights, a culture of human rights within the police organisation.

Until now, the Council of Europe has done substantial work on police training, human rights education for the police, police ethics and community policing. The Council of Europe, in cooperation with the Dutch police department and the Rotterdam police, last year organised a very useful multilateral conference on the subject of community policing.

Particularly in the last few years, the Council of Europe has devoted closer attention to the, sometimes burning, problems of minorities to community relations, and to the indispensable fight against racism and intolerance. The police have an important role to play in these respects. They have to adapt and to respond to the exigencies of the increasingly multi-cultural society in which we live. This is not an ideology, nor a doctrine. Whether we like it or not, it is reality. We live in a multi-cultural society in Europe today, and there is no point in denying or ignoring this reality. Any dream of an ethnically or religiously 'pure' society can only lead to a tragedy, as we witnessed in former Yugoslavia and particularly in Bosnia Herzegovina. In the Council of Europe we aim at dialogues between and understanding among cultures, for inter-cultural learning and education. The Vienna summit adopted a programme for confidence-building in civil society. I personally strongly disagree with Huntington's vision of the clashes of civilisations, which I find extremely dangerous; I do not accept that we are programmed for conflict between cultures and civilisations, and I do not want to accept that kind of determinism.[1] On the contrary, I believe that we must consciously fight the divisive and disruptive forces in our society and uphold what all human beings and communities have in common, what unites them, what is universal. Human rights are universal.

7. The human face of the police

Inter-cultural learning is necessary also for the police. The police will have to learn, and in many of our countries have learned, how to deal with different communities and with minorities. The police must also be close to citizens, whatever their origin. The police must have a face, they should not be faceless. In 1984, when he was still a dissident, Václav Havel, now President of the Czech Republic, wrote an excellent paper about the impersonal, anonymous bureaucratic power in totalitarian regimes. In a democratic society, state power, including that of the police, must be visible, must have a face, a human face. In its work concerning the police, the

---

[1]   See the lecture of M. Taylor in this publication.

17

Council of Europe wishes to work and does work with the police and its professional organisations, and it is looking forward to future cooperation with the international organisation of police chiefs. ELEC, the European Law Enforcement College, should be mentioned here. ELEC provides the Council of Europe with invaluable help in bringing the expertise of a democratic police to the countries of Central and Eastern Europe, and in promoting a non-political police in these countries that is based on the values of democracy, rule of law and human rights.

8. Conclusion

In conclusion, the aims of the Council of Europe can be summarised by the following three points:

1. The police must be seen as an essential element in a pluralist democracy based on the rule of law;

2. The police are a key actor in a democratic society;

3. The police should function as protector and promoter of human rights, or in other words: the police should be at the service of human rights.

For these aims to be achieved, the police need to be properly trained and educated. They need an ethos, they need ethics. In a Europe of pluralist democracy, the rule of law and human rights, we want to build together. It must essentially be what the distinguished Hungarian Janos Kish has called the ethics of the equal dignity of every human being, which is the foundation of the whole philosophy and law of human rights. Every human being in our society, which we want to be a democratic one, must be able to rely on the police for the defence of his or her fundamental rights and dignity.

5. POLICING WITHIN THE CONCEPT OF COMMUNITY POLICING

V.M. del Buono

1. The United Nations activities in crime prevention and criminal justice

The United Nations, since its foundation fifty years ago, has always had a programme of activities in crime prevention and criminal justice. In 1950, the General Assembly established an Ad Hoc Advisory Committee of Experts to advise the Secretary-General and the Social Commission of the Economic and Social Council on major policy directions in this area. In addition, the United Nations continued the practice it inherited from the League of Nations of holding large international congresses every five years to enable government delegations and a large and important non-governmental community to meet in order to formulate common or shared policies in various aspects of crime prevention or criminal justice. In 1955, for instance, the First Congress, held in Geneva, adopted the *Standard Minimum Rules for the Treatment of Prisoners*, which set out a series of standards and norms (rules) which countries should adopt for the treatment of their prisoners. The early congresses did considerable ground-breaking work in disseminating the results of experiments with new ideas in various fields of crime prevention and criminal justice – or social defence, as it was then termed.

2. The relation to law enforcement

The Third Congress, held in Stockholm in 1965, examined the scope of community preventive action (an early version of community crime prevention), and specifically the contribution that police services could make to the prevention of delinquency. This was 30 years ago. Police and other law enforcement officials and organisations have always played an important role in these discussions. The International Criminal Police Organisation prepared reports for both the Second and Third Congresses on the steps the police at that time were taking to win the confidence and co-operation of the public (in effect, policing in community policing).

In addition to this role of disseminating new ideas, the United Nations adopted some very important international instruments. These included *The 1975 Declaration on the Protection of all Persons from being Subjected to Torture and Other Cruel, Inhuman and Degrading Treatment or Punishment* which was incorporated into a *Convention Against Torture*. There is now an international committee that meets in Geneva and hears allegations against torture permitted or condoned by governments.

In 1979, the General Assembly adopted a resolution setting out a *Code of Conduct for Law Enforcement Officials*, which is a set of minimum standards for every law enforcement official in the world. The preamble sets out a series of guiding principles which bear reiteration, especially as they can serve as first principles for the discussion of community policing:

- *That, like all agencies of the criminal justice system, every law enforcement agency should be representative of and responsive and accountable to the community as a whole;*
- *That the effective maintenance of ethical standards among law enforcement officials depends on the existence of a well-conceived, popularly accepted and humane system of law;*
- *That every law enforcement official is part of the criminal justice system, the aim of which is to prevent and control crime, and that the conduct of every functionary within the system has an impact on the entire system;*
- *That every law enforcement agency, in fulfilment of the first premise of every profession, should be held to the duty of disciplining itself in complete conformity within the principles and standards herein provided and that the actions of law enforcement officials should be responsive to public scrutiny, whether exercised by a review board, a ministry, a procuracy, the judiciary, an ombudsman, a citizens' committee or any combination thereof, or any other reviewing agency;*
- *That standards as such lack practical value unless their content and meaning, through education and training and through monitoring, become part of the creed of every law enforcement official.*

In addition to this code of conduct and the *Guidelines for the Effective Implementation of the Code for Law Enforcement Officials* approved by the Economic and Social Council in 1989, the 1990 Eighth Congress adopted the *Guidelines for the Use of Firearms by Law Enforcement Officials*. At the fifth session of the new Commission on Crime Prevention and Criminal Justice (June 1996), Member States will consider a *Code of Conduct for Public Officials* which tackles issues related to corruption.

As was said at the outset, crime prevention and criminal justice have been the subjects of activity of the United Nations since its beginning. In 1991, there was a major renewal of the United Nations programme in this area, with a view to placing an additional emphasis on the implementation of the many standards and norms which were adopted in the first 40 years of the Programme. In addition to this enhanced role of coordinating the efforts of those countries who wish to provide each other with technical co-operation in crime prevention generally, and law enforcement, courts, and prisons specifically, the United Nations Crime Prevention and Criminal Justice Programme continues to play a very important role, now through the new Commission, in providing a forum in which Member States can come together to formulate common strategies in areas such as transnational organised crime, illegal use and importation of firearms, and corruption.

3. Interregional advisory services

Our principal function as interregional advisors is, when asked by countries, to provide advice on any problem or aspect of the criminal justice system, including law enforcement. We generally work with governments to help them improve their laws and criminal justice institutions, often mobilising international funding and expertise to assist them to do so. Since joining the United Nations 18 months ago, I have had occasion to examine, in some depth, aspects of law enforcement in several parts of the world including Pakistan, FYRO Macedonia, Kyrgyzstan, Argentina, and most recently South Africa. Those experiences, along with my experiences as a senior counsel of the Department of Justice in Canada, form the basis of the remarks made here on the subject of the policing within the concept of community policing.

4. Policing in the concept of community policing

The comments made here will be framed in the form of the kind of discussion that I am called upon at least three of four times a year to have with a Minister or Deputy Minister of the Interior who has requested the advice and assistance of the United Nations in transforming his country's police service into one which is more consistent with the democratic direction which his government wishes to take. This briefing is usually given at the end of a 'needs assessment' mission, during which a meeting is arranged with a number of persons and considerable documentation is studied to come to views as to what may need to be done.

The Minister, or his senior police official, has invariably heard something about an idea or set of ideas called 'community policing'. Both the Minister and the senior police officials wish for many reasons to enlist the support of the international community in their efforts, whether it is the United Nations or bilateral donors. They want both the know-how and modern techniques, and want their police service to think in line with 'modern' attitudes. They might also hope for some equipment at little or no cost from 'partners', for the reality is that in virtually all developing countries and countries in transition there is either no money, or not sufficient money, for innovation or improvement in the public sector at the time.

The desire to adopt 'community policing' (and the term can have many meanings) can be understood as a new and more democratic paradigm of law enforcement. It is attractive, perhaps, rhetorically compelling. However, the practice of community policing is the result of a long institutional, legal, and cultural history which, in the last analysis, may be very peculiar to Western European and North American society, and which may not be easily replicable in any other country – at least not without going through some of the same institutional developments that these countries have gone through.

The historical as well as the present political, economic and institutional contexts of Western Europe and North America and much of the rest of the world differ considerably. The first major difference has to do with the ethos of policing. An ethos is made up of a whole series of attitudes that take a long time to change. The recent history of the police in the five countries I mentioned, for example, is very different from that of Western Europe. Virtually all are emerging from a police culture which was decidedly militaristic. Probably the primary role of the police was the protection and preservation of the state and of those in power. Used as instruments of repression against their own people, they themselves were often victims of a repressive system, being poorly paid and enjoying few legal rights and standing. In addition, they were feared rather than respected, and now, because of this history, are still viewed at best with distrust and at worst with hatred.

In a culture of repression, such police forces relied heavily on the use of force, torture and a network of informers. They operated in a culture in which the 'Rule of Law' and legal institutions were weak, and where corruption, including the use of influence to affect the outcome of criminal cases, was a fact of life. Criminal cases often were based on confessions extracted by torture. As a practical consequence, these police forces seldom developed strong investigatory skills.

The political culture also was marked by a climate of repression, which sometimes was and sometimes was not effective in keeping levels of criminality down. In all cases, the move to democracy has brought in its wake a sharp increase in criminality, marked by high levels of violence against those with money. All these countries have experienced economic strains or downturns, which have included demands by the international banking industry for deep cuts in levels of government expenditure to reduce the size of the public sector.

These are a particular set of circumstances. Community policing is based on a very different evolution, ethos and set of circumstances. As a minimum, a 'professional' police force is a prerequisite, and that term encapsulates a great deal of law enforcement culture, history and values within it. It implies a long struggle to free police officers from partisan political control. It has meant a steady but substantial increase in the educational qualifications of those wanting to be police officers, in the salaries they are paid and in the other benefits they enjoy, including the rights to engage in some forms of union activity. It also meant that policing became a public service that was, and still is, very expensive.

The institutional and political context is also much different. Because reinforcing the state was one of the central functions of the police in developing countries and those in transition, they were invariably organised as large national organisations, centrally directed. In contrast, one of the other essential prerequisites of community policing is a strong local government with an independent tax-base that can sustain or at least substantially contribute to the cost of policing. Although there have always been concerns, especially in the American context, about the police being caught in municipal corruption if they become too financially dependent on municipal governments, I believe that 'community policing' must be based on some form of local financing, with the concomitant local accountability.

Community policing also has at its core the concept of service to citizens rather than the state. A citizen's identification with and support of the police stems from their service-functions rather than their law enforcement functions. A police officer who helps to take someone to the hospital, who directs a citizen to an appropriate governmental agency to solve a problem, or who does any of the other things officers do to help people, is thereby establishing links with people in the community. A necessary corollary of the above is that the police must have knowledge and understanding of the other public agencies' functions, and of the mode to access their services. Governments in developing countries are marked by a high degree of fragmentation. Although fragmentation is also present in developed countries, the level and number of social services which the police can assist in getting access to tends to be much greater.

For community policing to work there also must be a minimum level of social equality and social participation in civic affairs. If there are enormous differences in wealth, with a large majority of the population living below the poverty line, it would be difficult to see how public services – including policing – could be adequately funded. One of the things that those with money and property will always pay for, and thereby command a disproportionate societal share of, is the security to retain it.

Democratic policing (and community policing must be based on democratic institutions at both national and local levels) has at its core a series of interrelated tensions between the press, the politicians, the public, and the police. Learning to live with and manage those tensions is part of democratic government. One of the best guarantees of an effective police service is an active and free press. Even though sensationalist reporting of crime may be an irritation to those who have to manage the criminal justice system, this irritation is a small price to pay if the press is vigilant with respect to abuses of power by the police and dogged in exposing corruption. Abuse of power and corruption are not consistent with public control and accountability, and certainly would be inconsistent with community policing.

If these contextual factors exist, then community policing may be viable as a paradigm for policing. It may be that in a transitional period, as democratic government takes root, steps can be undertaken on the road to community policing. However, these will be at best interim measures until the necessary political and institutional frameworks for community policing are put in place.

5. The role of international organisations in a progress towards community policing

Slowly but surely, the involvement of international organisations in the field of security and justice is being accepted and their work recognised. Whether through the Crime Prevention and Criminal Justice Programme, or the United Nations Development Programme, which has primary responsibility for development within the United Nations system, or the Centre for Human Rights, which has applied many of the norms and standards our Programme has developed in the promotion and observance of human rights, the United Nations is assisting developing countries and countries in transition all over the world in shaping their criminal justice systems, reforming their constitutional and legal settings, and retraining their criminal justice personnel.

At present, there is a tremendous amount of international cooperation being undertaken bilaterally, and to a much lesser extent, multilaterally, in the area of policing. Most of this is useful in developing contacts between police forces, and in promoting a change of attitudes. However, institutional change, such as the introduction of community policing, requires a more long-term and developmental perspective, in which police officers, as substantive experts, do have an important role to play. That role can only be played successfully if undertaken in partnership with those working to change the broader context in which the police work.

The role of the criminal prevention and criminal justice system in development has been considered in many forums. In 1985 the Seventh Congress meeting in Milan adopted 47 guiding principles for crime prevention and criminal justice in the context of development and a new international economic order. Also, in 1990, the General Assembly in resolution 45/107 adopted 29 recommendations on international cooperation for crime prevention and criminal justice in the context of development. Both of these documents should be touchstones for the present flurry of initiatives in this area, and bear careful reading.

6. 'COMMUNITY' WITHIN THE CONTEXT OF COMMUNITY POLICING

M. Taylor

1. Introduction

Two very general points will be made in this chapter. The first concerns the police. It is in the nature of policing that when the legitimacy of the state, or the policing function, is challenged, the police ultimately have recourse to the use of non-negotiable force. This theme will be briefly discussed within a broader theoretical context, because it is a point which is often overlooked or diminished in discussions of community policing.

The second concerns society and communities. The nature of conflict is changing. We will see an increase in community-based violence, often related to a rejection of the legitimacy of the state. This will be dealt with within the broader context of terrorism as an example, though this example could have been organised crime as well.

These two issues are reciprocally related. As the state is rejected or questioned, the recourse to force on the part of the police will grow. The changed basis of conflict will present an enormous challenge to police forces, because they will bear the brunt of the problems on the streets. It must be admitted that a broadly pessimistic view of the future is presented here.

At the outset a fundamental position must be emphasised. The capacity to encourage and sustain supportive environments for police work must be a critical quality of the police function in democracies. The fundamental principle on which this paper is based is that the establishment and maintenance of a positive relationship between the police and the community is a necessary and essential element of the policing function. Sustaining such a relationship is the principle task that will face the police during what might be a time of increasing stress to the police forces of Europe.

First some topics in policing theory will be briefly explored. Police officers are usually very practical people, who regard theorising with great suspicion, the more so when it is done by an academic. Nevertheless, in this area there is nothing so practical as a good theory, because theories expose assumptions, and whether we like it or not, most of our activities are premised on assumptions and theories even though we do not recognise them.

2. Community policing: a dilemma

Despite many years of thinking about police work, its nature remains confusing. The term 'community policing' is even more confusing. It seems to have a lot in common with that other similar jargon phrase 'policing by consent' in requiring the questions 'Who? Whose community? Whose consent?' to be asked. But in a way these are strange questions to ask, because everyone is aware of the fact that policing can and does proceed in many places without the consent of the communities policed. It seems that community policing does not describe a clearly defined operational problem, to be solved by a technical process or some strategic intervention. Rather 'community policing' seems to be an expression of a central dilemma of policing. It is a dilemma which everyone can recognise, and for which solutions are sought. But because it is a fundamental dilemma, it is not so easy to find simple solutions. One element of this dilemma lies in the lack of clarity about the nature of police work. It might be helpful therefore to reflect on that for a moment.

Because the single word 'policing' is used to describe the activities of police officers, and because there is usually a single organisation to control them, one can easily be misled into imagining that the policing function is in some way a unified activity. In fact, police work is extraordinary heterogeneous. Indeed, so much so that there are grounds for giving some thought to whether all those tasks embraced within the police function should remain. A comparative European view on this is largely lacking, but would be of great value and interest.

Here, the context of the United Kingdom and Ireland will primarily be dealt with, although the analysis will probably extend to the police in other countries as well. The kind of activities the police undertake are in the main the result of complex historical and administrative forces, rather than rational and systematic planning. Police work can be identified as being derived from at least three sources:

- Some tasks are given to, or acquired by the police through a process of aggregation. These are the tasks which many social agencies might perform, but which the police either through accident or design, do provide. Perhaps this is because the police (or more likely their an-cestors) have always done them. Other tasks emerge because the po-lice as an arm of government and therefore an official state body are readily and cheaply available to perform some tasks. Because the po-lice as an organisation is widely distributed throughout a country, the use of the police in this way represents a cost-effective use of re-sources by the executive. In the past, the agricultural supervisory du-ties of the Irish Police force, the *Garda Siochanna*, are an example of this in Ireland. Perhaps some of the welfare roles of the police also fall into this category.

- Some tasks, however, are attracted to the police simply because they are there. The police are often the only 24 hours, 365 days per year widely available service in society. This, allied to the fact that the po-lice are a well trained and disciplined group, has resulted in the at-traction of activities such as helping people in distress, assisting in emergencies, etc. This might be termed task-creation by default. So-cial legislation, and the interface between social intervention of this kind and law enforcement creates particular strains here.

- Some tasks might, however, be argued to be unique to the police func-tion, as things which only the police can or should do. These unique tasks are in my view related to the relationship between the police and the state. They relate to order maintenance and law enforcement and effecting the wishes of the legislature, and in turn are crucially related to the powers of the police to arrest and regulate the actions of people. As Egon Bittner pointed out 25 years ago, these powers are premised on the essential capacity of the police and only the police to legiti-mately use force to ensure compliance, that force being non-negotiable as far as the recipient is concerned. Contemporary discus-sions of the social context of policing, within which the debate about community policing often takes place, frequently seem to largely evade this critical and distinctive issue. It is this capacity that seems to define those tasks which are unique to the police function, and which help us to both understand and set the scene for police behaviour on the street, as opposed to those tasks that other social agencies might perform. To identify such unique functions is not to devalue the other tasks the police may perform, but it does serve to establish a set of qualitatively different capacities and ultimately behaviour, which in some circumstances takes precedence over all others. Extreme situa-tions highlight this more general point.

29

In the light of this brief analysis, it can be seen why police work is so extraordinarily complex, and why police work encompasses tasks which might be mutually contradictory. This is obviously the case where order, maintenance or social welfare-related tasks conflict with law enforcement. But it can be seen in many other areas as well. Ordering priorities within so complex an array of activities presents obvious organisational, but more importantly, personal difficulties for individual police officers. We might also see this issue influencing the development of a particular kind of organisational culture. All of this relates to the capacity of the police (whether exercised or not in individual situations) to use non-negotiable force to effect compliance. Central to a concern with community policing is the missing equilibrium in the relationship between the police and the public which this creates, allied to the serious risk of an excessive concern with authority for both the individual police officer and the police organisation. A quite reasonable and understandable institutional response to this is to emphasise the importance of procedure and control as a means of constraining and focusing this considerable power. In turn, we can see how reactive rather than proactive strategies of policing will inevitably emerge through such processes of control and procedure. A further tension within this of course relates to discretion and in the British and Irish context, the office of constable, but these are matters to analyse further on another occasion.

3. Community policing and the capacity to use non-negotiable force

This short excursion into policing theory serves to establish the context to the rest of my paper. That which Bittner identified as the capacity to use non-negotiable force to effect compliance necessarily limits and constrains what can be achieved in community policing initiatives. From a psychological perspective, these constraints face the police officer on the ground with serious conflicts and stresses. Established psychological theory can help us to understand the nature of these difficulties, and perhaps indicate some of the solutions, but the fundamental nature of police work remains to limit what can be achieved.

It must be added that to identify constraints of this kind, which seem necessarily to set the police ultimately and necessarily in a position of authority over the public, does not imply that community-oriented qualities of police work should not be encouraged and developed. Rather, it is through recognising this essentially conceptual limitation to practical police work, that more realistic decisions about community policing initiatives could be made.

A controversial aside will be made here. The policing function does not necessarily depend on public support. The police can function very efficiently in some respects in the absence of such support, as anyone with a knowledge of a dictatorship will know. The grounding of police work both within the community and for the community is in a sense a political and historical choice which characterises police work in Europe and North America. But even in these countries ultimately the policing function must prevail if a state is to retain legitimacy.

4. Terrorism as a threat to democratic societies

This brings us to the issue of terrorism, and the second general point about the changing nature of conflict that was referred to in the introduction. It is of course precisely because of the need for the policing function to prevail that terrorism represents such an enormous threat to democratic societies, and another major stress for community involvement in policing can be identified. This can be examined in relation to the enormous changes that occurred in Eastern Europe. These changes have fundamentally called into question many of the basic assumptions about the nature of states, and about how societies might function. The changes are evident at both macro levels, in terms of the relations between states, and more significantly for our purposes at micro levels, in terms of how communities are made up, and the pressures they face.

One consequence of the immense changes in Eastern Europe has been not only that the influence of left wing ideologies has been greatly reduced, but that the whole notion of political ideologies as a driving force in human affairs has been greatly weakened. The imagery and rhetoric of the class struggle which so strongly characterised urban dissent since the 1960's has been debased, apparently leaving nothing obvious behind to replace it as a focus for political dissent. The moral and financial support by former Eastern block countries of West European terrorist and dissident groups has now ended. If the predominant ideological and financial supports are gone, will this mean the end of political terrorism and dissent as we have known it in Europe? If so, this would be significant indeed. After all, terrorism and political violence have been very powerful expressions of community disaffection, and have deliberately challenged police forces precisely at the community level.

The changes in Eastern Europe have liberated us from the widely-held assumption of the individual terrorist 'driven' by ideology to violence, a feature that does not of course accord with what is known about how actual terrorists behave. The time has come to think about terrorism in the same way that we think about other human behaviour. This is of some significance, for embedded in explanations of terrorist behaviour were psychological assumptions about what motivated people. Justifications of terrorist violence can now no longer claim legitimacy and draw upon disclaimers of moral and psychological responsibility by referring to either the inevitability of violence as a response to societies' insults, or to the ultimate 'political' correctness of their acts.

5. Terrorism and the community: clash of civilisations

Terrorism and its relationship with the community can now be more clearly examined for what it is, unobscured by political rhetoric and implied psychological assumptions. It seems that the most useful way of thinking about terrorism is to see it as a tool – a method to achieve certain ends amongst an array of other tools available to the activist. It is a tool which mobilises communities, challenges the authority of the state, and all too often draws the law enforcement community towards the development of repressive responses which, paradoxically, further serve to alienate and strengthen the terrorist group. The vicious circle of violence followed by what is perceived as repressive response quickly establishes a momentum of its own, generating and sustaining community-alienation. The awful reality is that terrorism is an effective weapon to challenge the state when the situation is appropriate. Terrorism begins when dissent stops being peaceful, and it targets either the political process directly, or the media. In doing this it has a primary aim of disturbing the sense of well-being of a community. The Chinese proverb '*kill one, frighten ten thousand*' captures the emotional and essentially psychological effect the terrorist seeks to achieve. It also clearly places terrorism within the community, and helps us to understand how through what might be characterised as intimidation, it is an important factor shaping and limiting the relationship between the police and the community.

It has been argued that the changes in Eastern Europe represent a change in the basic paradigm that is applied to understand the relations between communities and states, and perhaps more generally to the way the origins and sources of conflict at all levels should be seen. Most notably, Huntington has proposed an alternative way of thinking about how our world is structured, and particularly has offered us what he regards as a new paradigm to understand how conflicts in the world will develop. In his important paper in 1993 in Foreign Affairs, '*The Clash of Civilisations*' he analyses what he regards as being the sources of conflict in the changed world. He argues that '*...the fundamental sources of conflict in this new world will not be primarily ideological or primarily economic. The great divisions among humankind and the dominating source of conflict will be cultural.*' In his view '*...the fault lines between civilisations will be the battle lines of the future*'.

In a European context, he suggests that the most significant 'fault' line may well follow the Eastern boundary of Christianity in 1500. This line runs along what are now the borders of Finland and Russia, between the Baltic States and Russia, cuts through Belarus and the Ukraine, separating Transylvania from the rest of Rumania, and then goes through the former Yugoslavia, separating Slovenia from Croatia, and largely follows the line of conflict in Bosnia and Herzegovina.

By civilisation, Huntington means a cultural entity – '*...the highest cultural grouping of people and broadest level of cultural identity people have*' – a grouping that extends beyond regions and nations. He defines a civilisation in terms of '*...common objective elements, such as language, history, religion, customs, institutions, and by the subjective self-identification of people.*' He recognises that people have levels of identity related to a locality, a state, a religious sect (Roman Catholic, Protestant), a religion (Islam, Christianity), ethnicity, a multi-state entity (a European) or a broad conceptual entity such as a Westerner or an African. What Huntington means by a civilisation is the broadest level of identification with which an individual intensely identifies. People can and do redefine their identities, and because of the boundaries and composition of 'civilisations' these can change. Whilst asserting that states will remain the most powerful actors in world affairs, Huntington places greater emphasis on civilisations as broader and more fundamental entities that will drive conflict.

Recent wars have of course at one level been about territories, raw materials and money. But, according to Huntington, they have more importantly been fundamentally about what the theologian Hans Küng has termed the '*underlying ethnic and religious structures*' of civilisations. What perhaps Huntington has done most of all is to draw our attention to the deeper cultural (and essentially community) dimensions of current conflicts. In the European context, these fundamental forces were of course always there, but until recently our attention has been focused on what might be thought of as the technical facilitators of violence (such as relative poverty, social oppression, etc.). The recent political changes in Europe have allowed us to become more aware of the more significant fundamental processes. Huntington's chilling assessment of the future is that, '*The next world war, if there is one, will be a war between civilisations*'.

The fundamental feature of civilisations is not political affiliation, but religion, or perhaps more broadly, culture, and the 'fault lines' in the world (including Europe) will in this view increasingly relate to the age-old frontiers between religions and confessions. If this is the case, it can be seen why countries that are made up of aggregations of different 'civilisations' (such as the former Soviet Union or former Yugoslavia) will feel pressures towards breaking up. Similarly, countries which have some measure of cultural unity (such as Mexico and Turkey) but are internally divided about which 'civilisation' they belong to, will also experience great difficulty. Some parts of the USA may fall within this category, as might be the case with Canada.

Huntington views have been criticised, and it would not be appropriate here to debate at length the merits of specific elements of his ideas. What is important about Huntington's views for our purposes is that he gives us a basis from which to think about the future, and from the specific perspectives of this paper, gives us a way in which we can begin to see how the psychological and cultural focuses of conflict at a community level, including terrorism, might arise now that the major East-West divisions no longer seem to apply in the same way. In a sense, the significance of what Huntington is saying is that it offers us another set of polarities around which political dissent can be structured and understood. These forces are the factors that influence and shape our communities, and in policing terms, these forces need to be understood to effectively relate policing to community aspirations and structures.

There can be no doubt at all that as a tool within broader conflicts, terrorism will continue to flourish and develop. But rather than seeing terrorism as the instrument of ideological struggle (of the left or right), we will see the growth of terrorism related to what Huntington calls 'civilisations' as an element in a broader concept of warfare, and as an element in more local symptoms of broader conflicts. In addition, we might witness a rise in terrorism related to inter-civilisation disputes sometimes for the reasons Küng suggests as '*torn countries*', sometimes because of more straightforward disputes over power or money (which might sometimes relate to criminality and organised crime), and sometimes because of a strongly-held ideology or moral views (which might, for example, relate to single-issue terrorism related to the environment, animal rights, etc.). All of these various facets of political violence will happen because terrorism is and remains an attractive tool for disaffected groups and groupings to exercise a disproportionate influence. These are the forces which police organisations will increasingly have to face and understand, because these will form the bases for the community tensions in extreme situations which the police will have to face in attempting to maintain law and order.

This general theme can be developed by taking an example. Thinking in terms of the fault-lines of Europe, many of Huntington's and Küng's ideas can be seen to be working themselves out in the Balkans. Serbian, Croatian and Bosnian identity seem increasingly to be related to religious affiliation, and these irreconcilable differences in identity are undoubtedly significant factors driving the conflict. These differences survived the state of Yugoslavia and have surfaced with surprising strength. Whilst individual Bosnians, for example, may well resist their characterisation as Muslims, any visitor to Sarajevo and Central Bosnia rapidly becomes aware of the increased 'Islamisation' of Bosnian society. I first began to visit Sarajevo over three years ago, and I have become aware of the growth in the number of Mosques, and the increased number of women wearing Islamic dress in the city. From discussions with women there, I know that for some, the wearing of a veil is a statement of their religious values, but for others it is a statement of national identity as a Bosnian. The 'old', 'conventional' political ideologies do little to help us to understand these changes, or this conflict.

Was the Bosnian conflict an example of terrorism and what does it tell us about policing a community? From the perspective of NATO and IFOR, and UNPROFOR before these, it was a war, and required the response of large-scale military intervention (as could be seen in the air strikes). Similarly, I do not doubt that the governments of the states involved currently see the conflict in terms of warfare. But at another level, it seems that the Bosnian conflict may represent not only an example of Huntington's ideas working out, but also as a more general example of a future form of terrorism and community violence. For as experienced by the citizens of Sarajevo, they have been subjected by the warring states to what amounts to a series of extensive systematic terrorist attacks which in its effects are like those of a sustained terrorist campaign, except on a scale we have never recently experienced before. The war in Bosnia has in the main not been characterised by large scale fighting by armies in recent times, but by many small scale individual attacks primarily targeted at civilians. Instead of car bombs (as, for example, the Provisional IRA used in London), the explosions have been through shelling; and individual attacks on civilians have been made through sniping.

The psychological qualities of this (and in my view it is this feature that makes elements of this conflict an example of terrorism), at least as it relates to Sarajevo, can be illustrated by some of the observations made by my co-workers in the city. Up to the cease-fire in early 1994, around 1–2 children on average were killed daily in the city. Of those deaths and of injuries sustained by children, between a fifth and a quarter were the result of bullet wounds, a consequence of sniping. Injury through sniping, unlike the injuries caused by shrapnel, is not random; it requires a deliberate act in aiming the weapon. This, and other evidence, suggests that children have been deliberately targeted in this conflict. The reason for this is not because children have some role in the conflict per se, but presumably because targeting them is seen as an effective way of producing fear and despondency amongst the population at large. As experienced by the citizens of the warring states, this war has been almost personalised to the local communities involved.

6. Refugees within the community

This brings us back to the main themes of this paper, and to an issue of direct relevance to community issues in policing. As a result of the fighting in former Yugoslavia, and of the more general economic and social tensions in Eastern Europe, we are seeing a great rise in the numbers of refugees in Europe. Most major European urban areas have large East-European refugee populations. Most of these refugee communities have made little effort to integrate with the broader community, and they have retained their original ethnic and social identity. In addition, there are good grounds for suggesting that organised criminal elements are playing an increasing role in the fabric of these communities. If Huntington's analysis is correct, these communities may well serve as the vehicle for exporting their own tensions and conflicts to other parts of Europe. I have no wish to scapegoat these communities, but they undoubtedly will in my view serve as a pool from which potential political and criminal violence might develop. Both are already beginning to be associated with these communities. The relationship between immigrant communities and political violence are already clear in some examples of Islamic terrorism which draw upon immigrant communities, and there is no reason why the same should not be the case with respect to European tensions. Similarly, we are well aware of the activities of organisations like the PKK, who are heavily involved in money-laundering and extortion amongst their own communities. Perhaps this more than anything represents the extension of this analysis into issues related to community policing. For many of these ethnic groups represent profound challenges to our concepts of consent and shared community values on which our models of democratic policing are based.

7. Conclusion

How does all this relate to our concepts of community policing? What do the relationships between states or even civilisations have to do with the essentially local issues involved in urban policing? I believe they have a great deal to do with these, because it is these large forces that condition how communities and individuals relate to authority and the law. At one level community policing may be about sustaining local relationships and a sense of cohesion and community well-being. I am well aware that from a policing perspective it may also be about the mobilisation of community support in areas such as crime-prevention. But in areas of social or political stress, the central issues discussed above transcend more local agendas and do impinge on the broader social and cultural context.

To bring this paper to a conclusion, the problems identified here do not diminish the value of community policing-initiatives, nor reduce a commitment to the development of an increased measure of sensitivity of the police to community concerns. Quite the reverse, it is only by firmly grounding the police in the broader community that we can hope to weather some of the stresses we now see on the horizon in our urban areas. This is not the place to discuss ways in which police forces must move to address these problems, other than to suggest the route lies in a greater awareness and acceptance of the maintenance of human rights as a central core of the police function. What I hope I have done is to at least identify some of the problems that we face. Later papers will address more strategic and operational experiences. But I do not believe it is exaggerating the position to say that the qualities of our democracies that we value depend on the successful matching of the police function to community need. It is a task we must not fail in.

7. POLICING 2000. BALTIMORE AND THE PRACTICE OF COMMUNITY POLICING

T.C. Frazier

1. Community policing in Baltimore

In Baltimore, we have put into place a well-defined and very focused Community Policing Plan, one that places quality of life for citizens at the very heart of the plan. Significant resources are devoted to ensuring that officers and supervisors understand the plan, its methods, and its goals. To that end, each officer and supervisor in the department has received and will continue to receive focused training to ensure that everyone is working from the same page. In essence, here is how Community Policing is defined in Baltimore:

Police and law-abiding citizens work together to do four things:

- arrest offenders;

- prevent crime;

- solve on-going problems;

- improve the quality of life in the community.

Every sworn officer in the city has been trained in the use of these principals, and every officer is fully engaged in 'community policing'. Different deployment-models are being tried in districts throughout the city in an effort to find the best organisational and tactical approach to applying these models to everyday tasks. Working together with other city agencies to provide coordinated services to fight the 'crime and grime' issues which so adversely affect the citizen's perception of order and safety is another important issue here.

To provide a focused tool to more directly combat the upward trend of violent crime, the Violent Crime Task Force (VCTF) was created. Its main objective is the reduction of violent crime involving firearms and the illegal possession of hand-guns. The VCTF, part of the Criminal Investigation

Bureau, operates city-wide, independent of, but in cooperation with, officers and commanders from each of the nine police districts.

In its first initiatives, the VCTF identified and focused on the three areas of the city with the highest incidence of violent crime and the greatest problem with 'open air drug markets'. The following carefully planned strategy was implemented in these three areas of the city:

- Suspects were identified and observed over several weeks.

- Suspects were indicted, and warrants with pre-set bails were obtained.

- Large scale raids, or 'sweeps', of each area were made, with mass arrests and numerous gun-, cash- and narcotic-recoveries made.

- Almost simultaneously, other city agencies came in and boarded up or demolished vacant houses, cleaned up vacant lots, alleys and streets, and covered up graffiti, to restore the area to neighbourhood use.

The VCTF has been a major building block in Baltimore's community policing effort, as attested to by the fact that after each sweep-operation, neighbourhood residents cheered the officers and what they were doing.

As a result of these efforts, violent crime in these neighbourhoods was dramatically reduced, and a new sense of cooperation and renewed sense of hope was born. In the area of the first sweep-operation, violent crime last year was down 42% – well over a year after the 'sweep' actually occurred.

To further reduce crime throughout the city, Shooting Investigation Squads were created within the VCTF. These teams follow up all shooting incidents throughout the city, on a 24-hour-a-day basis. All shootings are considered as actually unsuccessful homicides, and a centralised, coordinated, well-trained cadre of investigators, such as is devoted to murder cases is seen as the best approach to solve these crimes.

Six million guns are purchased each year in the United States half of them are hand-guns. Furthermore two million guns are stolen each year in the U.S. These facts, and our knowledge of the prevalence of hand-gun-related crimes and of illegally possessed hand-guns has prompted the creation of Gun Recovery Squads within the VCTF. These squads are equipped with hand-held metal detectors, and their singular task is to detect and recover illegal guns and arrest violators. In this mission they use not only the metal detectors, but they are specially trained to observe subjects and detect nuances of behaviour that indicate illegal gun-possession.

As indicators of the success of this approach in the last three years, the following can be mentioned: since community policing was first put into effect, shooting dropped by 30% (730 fewer incidents) in 1994 compared to 1993, and the number for 1995 was roughly the same as 1994. Gun seizures city-wide for the first two months of 1993 and 1996 are up 26.4%, while violent crime has been reduced by 1.7%.

2. Five key strategies

Over the next several years, five key strategies are set forth for the Department:

1.   Increase the number of officers in direct crime-fighting positions;

2.   Emphasise activities directed at gun-violence and gun-seizures;

3.   Retake the city's public spaces;

4.   Build partnerships, that is to say join forces with law-abiding citizens to strengthen the city's neighbourhoods block by block;

5.   Curb future crime activity through an expanded Police Athletic League.

More officers on the street

The primary goal of the Baltimore Department for 1996 is to assign more sworn police personnel to direct crime-fighting duties. Our goal is to add another 184 to the 159 additional officers assigned in 1995 for a total of 2,566 crime fighters on the street. This increase will be accomplished through the redeployment of sworn officers from administrative to direct positions in the Field Operations and Criminal Investigation Bureaux, and enhanced recruitment and training.

The slimming down process at police headquarters and in the police districts will result in a significantly higher number of officers on the streets – where they belong.

Focus on gun-related crime

In 1996 gun-related crime will be vigorously combated on multiple fronts, primarily through refocusing patrol priorities, expanding investigation and increasing gun seizures.

In the past, too much of the officers' time has been spent on making low-level drug arrests. Every drug arrest involves officers in a four-hour booking process, which results in few meaningful convictions and a negligible impact on street violence. Obviously, an officer on the street is more

41

effective in maintaining order and denying the opportunity for violence than an officer spending hours in a booking facility.

This is not to say drug distribution organisations, large and small, will not continue to be targeted. They certainly will be. It is to say that street addicts with small amounts of narcotics will no longer be an enforcement priority.

Gun seizures are also a key tactic in our effort against gun-related violence. In the last two years, this agency has taken in approximately 6,500 guns, through arrests and gun turn-in programs. Three initiatives will increase gun seizures in 1996.

Already one additional Gun Recovery Unit is added to the Violent Crime Task Force. Both units will be staffed with a sergeant and eight police officers. Their primary objective will be to reduce the incidence of gun violence through aggressive detection and recovery of illegal firearms before they are used.

Second, all sworn members of the agency are receiving additional training in the laws of arrest, search and seizure and in identifying certain behavioural characteristics exhibited by persons who are armed. Our patrol members will be able to observe and recognise these tendencies and will be able to articulate reasonable suspicion to justify a stop-and-frisk. To assist in reasonable stop-and-frisk, we are utilising the specialised 'frisk wands'. These wands are essentially hand-held metal detectors which identify weapons in a less intrusive manner than the traditional manual frisk.

Third, we will communicate to law-abiding citizens how they can assist the Department's gun seizures through our widespread '*See a Gun, Call 911*' advertising campaign, donated by a local advertising company.

Through increased personnel, training, equipment, communication and incentives, I am confident we will continue to substantially increase gun seizures this year.

Retaking public space

When thinking of crime, generally an individual victim comes to mind. However, a neighbourhood can be a victim, whenever crimes such as prostitution, purse-snatching and even vandalism in the form of graffiti occur. The cumulative result of criminal activity is a neighbourhood with decreased property values, diminished quality of life, and pockets of abandonment. This year, the Baltimore police force will work to maintain order and safety in public spaces – the parks, greenways and commercial areas – that are central to the city's well-being.

To this purpose, a Street Crimes Unit is created, consisting of a lieutenant, two sergeants and 24 officers, whose priority is crimes against the neighbourhood. This special unit will work both in uniform and plain-clothes operations, enforcing laws ranging from street robbery to aggressive panhandling, and providing prevention through street-corner visibility and apprehension through decoy investigations. We will also work with the courts to ensure that crimes against the community are addressed immediately and directly.

Regaining territory block by block

The nine district commanders now have real authority and responsibility for their individual districts. They are in charge of directing their resources in their districts strategically, identifying strong blocks and extending the strengths found there to 'convert' adjacent blocks. In particular, the commanders and officers must draw upon the resource of caring, active individuals within the community.

On an informal basis, concerned citizens influence their fellow neighbours to keep up their homes, alleys and streets, as well as cooperating with police to prevent and solve crimes. This year, the efforts of these individuals will be supported and others will be recruited into service through a pro-active Block Representative Program. We have already begun to provide block-representatives with a comprehensive package of guidelines to enable them to perform an effective leadership role on their individual blocks. Community-leaders will be worked with to stimulate interest in the programme and conduct training.

Police officers do understand the importance of a supportive community in preventing and solving crimes in the city's neighbourhoods. No police department can ever have enough officers to do the job alone. Our goal is to build a cadre of thousands of dedicated block representatives who are well prepared to work with district officers to make and keep their neighbourhoods strong.

Prevention through the Police Athletic League

We know that it takes a significant number of officers to control an unruly crowd of, say, 25 juveniles, while putting both the police and the juveniles at risk of injury. We also know that a single police officer, working as part of a well-designed and implemented Police Athletic League Program (PAL), can gain the trust and divert the energies of dozens of juveniles, thereby helping to prevent the formation of a large disorderly crowd in the first place.

43

PAL provides structured activities to bring officers together with the city's youth for non-adversarial, positive interaction. In the natural and enjoyable context of sports and other recreational activities, officers work to provide a good influence on the lives of these young people. It is firmly believed that, over time, the trust and respect fostered between police officers and the youth of our community will pay an ongoing dividend by reducing juvenile crime. The investment in PAL today will help reduce the high costs of crime – both human and monetary – tomorrow.

In 1995, PALs were established in each of the nine District Offices. This year, it is an intention to expand the programme into additional sectors across the city. Providing safe spaces, positive activities and good role models is a job that no other organisation can do better than the Baltimore Police Department.

We will continue to establish effective programs aimed at diverting our youth toward positive activities, to provide positive role-models and mentoring programs, and to establish opportunities for our police officers and the youth of our city to work together to solve problems, build pride in one another, and reclaim a generation that, according to some, is already lost.

Additionally, there are several other areas where we will concentrate our efforts over the next ten years in trying to keep up with the ever-changing challenges facing law enforcement.

Use of advanced technology

A significant expansion of the use of computers and PC networks to further enhance data access, data sharing and communications has already been started. Mobile Work Stations have been installed in each of the marked police units. Automation of the Offence-Reporting process is currently being planned, and we are looking at eventually moving to direct crime/incident data entry by patrol officers into laptop computer systems throughout the patrol force. Together, these automation strategies will greatly enhance the timeliness, accuracy, and volume of crime and incident data, and therefore aid our prevention and investigatory efforts.

De-emphasising 911

In the vast majority of the United States, citizens in trouble contact their local police-department by simply dialling three digits – 911 – instead of the usual 7 digits. But we have oversold this quick and simple way to notify the police, and for some years now we have observed that people seem to know and use no other number for the police. So that whenever they want to contact the police, even for simple administrative purposes, they call 911, which is specifically designed to speed a marked police unit toward an address. Worse still, more and more people call 911 for virtually any problem they have with any city agency.

As a result, every day our officers 'chase 911 calls'. And yet we know that many of the calls they respond to could be better handled by other departmental resources, or even by other city agencies. This is the result of years of overuse of the 911 emergency number by our citizens for non-emergency, and often non-police, purposes. We are now beginning to use advertising which de-emphasises the use of 911, as well as certain new technologies, to identify and divert all non-emergency calls to other departmental resources, or, when appropriate, resources outside the department.

3. Conclusion

Let me conclude by emphasising that the crime, disorder and financial problems faced in Baltimore are not unique to our city, to our country, or even to our continent. We understand that virtually all of these many problems have been, are, or will be facing each city and country represented here today. Indeed, if not universal, these problems are at least global in nature and scope. Which is the reason for a conference such as this one, where common problems can be discussed, and more importantly, our perspectives shared.

8. THE PRACTICE OF COMMUNITY POLICING IN THE ROTTERDAM-RIJNMOND REGION

R.H. Hessing

1. Introduction

Community policing is more than just a vogue word by which the police today want to express their involvement in and responsibility for a secure community. Community policing is also more than a movement based on pious intentions or ideological concepts of a security policy. Community policing is a practical and realistic approach, in which the organisational set-up and the performance of police tasks is tailored to the smallest possible geographical areas matching the public's living environment and within which the public's security is of vital importance.

2. The history of community policing

The development of today's community policing in the Netherlands and in Rotterdam may be explained largely from the history of the police during the past thirty years, or more particularly, the history of the police organisation, which mainly resulted from political and administrative views of how the police should perform their tasks.

From a historical perspective, four periods can be distinguished:

- the period of the fifties and sixties, when traffic problems were the central issue;

- the period of the late sixties and seventies, strongly influenced by the approach towards law and order problems and large-scale police actions;

- the late seventies and eighties, when the relationship between the police and the community was the central theme, and

- since the late eighties and early nineties we have been fully engaged in the debate on how the police can best shape and realise the relationship between the police and the public, and which organisational concept is the most appropriate for that purpose.

This debate has increasingly set the concept of community policing. During these periods, the internal organisation of the police has followed these developments. During the periods when traffic order, public order and law enforcement were the central issues, the police service was a compartmentalised organisation. The police organisation was characterised by a separated, compartmentalised, vertical department structure.

There were usually three separate departments working side by side: one for traffic, one for patrolling and guarding, and a criminal investigation department for the fighting of crime. At that time, police thinking was also dominated by sector thinking, and problems were reduced to one of these three sectors.

3. Community policing: a new ideological and organisational concept

The sharp rise in crime in the early eighties prompted a fundamental debate in this country about the task of the police and their organisation. This debate was characterised by an ideological aspect and an organisational one.

The central theme in the ideological aspect was that the activities of the police should not only be repressive, directed exclusively at law and order, but that further, and certainly to the least extent, they should be directed at the quality of life and the security of the community in which the police work. Furthermore it was emphasised that the police, too, had to ensure that the rights and freedoms of individuals and groups were respected.

In order to follow that road, it was necessary to have police forces which did not merely have a judicial attitude, but which filled the role in the local community, visibly and daily, of guarding and protecting, of the attentive and active public servant of the community which wished to be protected and assisted.

Apart from all the organisational problems, this called for a police service working alongside and among the citizens in the community, both literally and mentally. In such a concept, the police are not just present, the public actually experiences the police as being their police. This ideological concept was indicated in the eighties as the road to be taken in the future, and this ideology still forms one of the pillars of community policing today.

The organisational concept was directed at ending the compartmental-ised organisation based on separate departments. Putting an end to com-partmentalisation also meant that the centralist set-up, central command and central control of the police effort had to be abandoned as well. The new key words that were introduced were: integration (of tasks) and de-centralisation (of the performance of tasks). In addition, the large-scale set-up of the police organisation had to be replaced by a small-scale structure.

Surroundings-oriented work, or rather area-oriented work was adopted as a new concept for the police. The organisations were changed. Area-oriented work formed the starting-point for setting up the new units. Within them, as regards the performance of tasks, the concept of Basic Police Care was elaborated upon. The maximum number of police tasks was to be performed by the maximum number of police officers. This was a sort of generalist U-turn, with only the very specific tasks to be per-formed by central specialists. Parallel to this development, a new view of the public was adopted. The public increasingly came to be seen as the consumer of police products, as client and partner. This added to the proc-ess of area-oriented work, and also gave rise to the notion that a police or-ganisation must remain flexible and can never be static.

So the introduction of area-oriented working did not mean an end to the development of the police organisation. It rather formed the basis, the starting-point from which to shape and realise a new future. Area-oriented work provided the basis for further thinking, a fine-tuning, to further ex-pand the relationship between the police and the community. Community policing is the dynamic result of that process. In our work today, commu-nity policing especially concerns the role of the police and the organisa-tional set-up is a result.

Community policing means that the police must make sure that they are available, known and accessible. Proximity of the police contributes to a sense of security, the need for which is felt very deeply by society. By their integrated method of working, the police should respond vigilantly to criminal offences without claiming to be capable of influencing crime substantially.

Together with the public, the police should support the public's own power to keep their surroundings manageable. In addition, the police should be the driving force of a strategic alliance between police, local government, public service departments and social institutions, in order to tackle acute problems in districts or neighbourhoods by means of coop-eration and targeted action. Before entering into the organisational details of the concept of community policing, I should first make a number of observations about the context of the police task.

4. The public's security as a main theme: adaptation to local circumstances and cooperation

The task of the police may be described as contributing to the community's security by entering into or performing arrangements which more specifically aim to increase the security of the public.

When looking at everyday practice, we find that the performance of this task mainly involves tackling or solving specific problems; security problems which, in the eyes of the public, urgently need to be dealt with, and in which the potential of exercising power or exerting coercion plays a major role.

The police are thus concerned with a wide variety of activities, ranging from giving assistance in emergencies, advising, corrective action, repression, supervision, detection and so forth.

What is characteristic is that the question as to which of these activities is to be performed and the way in which they are to be performed strongly depends on the situation. The problems that have to be dealt with, the decision as to what the public themselves can or cannot do and where they need support, differ from situation to situation. The added value given by the police lies in their ability to develop 'live' arrangements which respond to those various contexts. These arrangements define what is expected from the police and what the police commit themselves to. Their content always depends on local circumstances and therefore depends on both time and place.

Apart from actually contributing to the implementation of arrangements, the police also play a supporting role for the other partners. Partners in these arrangements are: the local authorities, the public prosecution service, social institutions and the public. It will always be a mixture, directed at specific problems. A matter of concern here is the fact that everybody works from their own perceptions, their own angles. All these different angles have to be matched so as to produce manageable links.

The police may be expected to play an intermediary role here, and their duty is to match the divergent expectations. Against this backdrop, it would be useless to formulate exhaustive descriptions of the task of the police. Anyone who recognises that the police operate within a rationality determined by the situation will have to realise that fixing a task, without referring to local arrangements in doing so, will only create new fictions.

The arrangements define the expectations which the other partners may cherish with respect to the police, and they describe the responsibilities borne by the police. To a large extent, the role of the police derives from the arrangements within the normative limits to which they are bound in performing their task.

Exactly the same may be said about, for instance, the health service. The specific nature, however, is that the police also aim to assist others in enforcing the norms leading to security. Irrespective of whether they assist, inform, correct or prevent, that is their dominant feature.

Drawing up arrangements always requires a basis. These are not paper plans, but agreements to act in a certain manner in a certain situation. Making arrangements is not easy, because each time the prerequisite is that agreements can only be made if they can actually be complied with by the parties.

5. Policing, a paradoxical activity

The quality of security in our society is threatened not only by those who break the norms, but also by all sorts of acts which encourage the breaking of norms or reduce the self-regulating power of the public. The latter is also done by the government, by claiming that 'the government is responsible for security'. This implies that policing is a paradoxical activity.

On the one hand, the government should promote security or even guarantee it by taking action itself. On the other hand, the government should promote the concept that the public and social institutions also take on their own responsibility, and that the government takes no action itself and remains passive. As a government body, the police are trapped in that paradox. This paradox can only be broken when the police empower other parties rather than seeking to increase their own power.

For the police, the implications of all this are by no means minor. They develop their relations with the public in a sense of involvement with society. They register the effects of their own actions and those of others. First and foremost, this means openness at all levels, even when this creates tensions. It also means debates about how far the police can go in their social involvement.

As a result of their actual emphasis on prevention and innovation, police officers are now seen to devote themselves to training- and employment-projects to protect criminal youngsters from slipping down further. Police officers are also involved in the allocation of homes, and they act as intermediaries in the job market. The point is not whether this is right or wrong, whether this is allowed or not allowed; what matters is the continued debate about where the limits are.

In this context, community policing may also be described as the striving for synthesis between the professionalism of the organisation and the external orientation in applying it. The central theme here is: how can we ensure the creative and flexible gearing of police activities to what is happening in the surroundings? Will the police succeed in regulating the public's expectations without displaying the limitation of their possibilities as a weakness?

6. The four pillars of community policing in Rotterdam

In the Rotterdam-Rijnmond police organisation, community policing is based on four pillars.

The first pillar consists of making arrangements with our strategic partners. Reference was made to this in some detail earlier on. Arrangements are a cooperation model in which the partners complement and reinforce each other. We are seeking 'complementariness', aimed at an overall security policy geared to the local community. The starting-point is to realise a coherent package of measures. Apart from supplying their own specific input, the police also play a directing role here.

The second pillar is that the field of action of the police is seen as one whole. The problems are interrelated. The public's sense of security is determined by an accumulation of big and small problems. It is a matter of plus-plus-plus: not just the stolen car radio or bicycle, but also the graffiti, the burglary, the serious crimes, the seemingly insoluble drug problems, the lack of respect for the red traffic light and parking restrictions, and so on and so forth. All these aspects together determine the sense of insecurity. These things are interrelated, and thus leave little room for the decision to disregard some of these matters. Not dealing with them or tolerating them, whether or not for lack of time, breaches the credibility of the government and, in the end, the credibility of the police.

The interrelation of things demands an overall response by the police themselves, the third pillar. This means that the police product, or what we offer as a response to the problems as a whole, must also be coherent. So they can never be isolated products. Here, the plus-plus-plus principle also applies. Even organised crime starts at street corners: the small-time drug dealers, the foreign exchange dealer, the gangland punishment, the cafe where stolen property is bought and sold. In brief, wherever the individual policeman goes, he will meet with organised crime. And where the police explicitly fight organised crime, they are concerned with the public's security. Enforcing traffic rules (the red light, the speed limit, parking restrictions) contributes to a sense of norms and to the confidence in the law in general.

In general, the impression made by law enforcement is deeply underrated – and wrongly so. When we in Rotterdam today, in the context of neighbourhood security and community policing, say 'clean, whole and secure', we mean clean, orderly surroundings where people abide by the rules. We have learned that these three concepts, 'clean, whole and secure', largely determine the public's sense of security.

The fourth pillar is, briefly, that the police should go to the public. One shouldn't wait until problems actually occur, but networks should be built which allow the police to be one step ahead of the problems and to prevent them. We write INTRICATE POLICE STRUCTURE in capitals. It should be tailored to districts and neighbourhoods. It can only be achieved when we make police officers individually responsible for very small areas. Of course, that is a relative responsibility, as the size of a small area is related to the population factor and the security problems. Naturally, in a suburb or a villa area an intricate police structure will differ from that in an inner-city slum area with high unemployment. From an organisational point of view, there will always be differentiation and flexibility, but the basic principle of how we work remains the same.

7. Intricate police structure and personal involvement

In our concept of community policing we try to reconcile two starting-points. These are an intricate police structure and the police officer's personal involvement. Currently, experiments are being executed with various models of intricate police structure, to organise the work as close to the public as possible. Structures are looked for which allow the police to work among the public. This means that the organisation is divided into small units which, as it were, are supposed to work as a kind of feelers extended into the community. Broadly speaking, a model is envisaged in which police officers work in small groups that are responsible for arranging security and providing daily police care in a small area. Depending on the (demographic) situation, this may be a few streets, a neighbourhood, or a district. For the sake of convenience, the neighbourhood level will be referred to in the rest of this paper. These small groups of police officers work from a police post in the neighbourhood. These police posts have been set up in houses that were made available (a living-room sized police post), or in empty shops. Experiments have also been set up with curb-side police posts, and a grocer's van has been converted into a mobile police post. Police shopping is another new aspect of community policing. The main task of the small-scale police posts is to reduce frequently occurring forms of crime. Alongside this, they are charged with raising and maintaining the quality of life in the neighbourhood (combating nuisance). They do not do that on their own, but in close cooperation with other strategic partners with whom arrangements are made.

This approach requires a different type of police officer. Of course the police officer will continue to catch crooks and maintain law and order, but in addition he will have to develop into being a 'networker', of whom great social involvement is demanded. Establishing close contacts with the residents in his neighbourhood is the only way of being in the midst of the community. The neighbourhood knows him. He is recognisable, he is always accessible and available. Round the clock. Conversely, he also knows his neighbourhood: local nuisance, local crime, the problem families, the schools, the catering establishments, et cetera. The point is 'knowing and being known'. We have introduced the concept of the 'family officer', who may, in some respects, be compared to the family doctor. The family doctor has a limited number of patients. His patients know him and he knows his patients. The family officer can build up a relationship of trust with a neighbourhood and with its residents. Catching crooks will always continue to be the core business of the police, but in addition we wish to acquire a pivotal role in the community.

For the public, the family officer must develop into a sort of 'help desk' for lots of different problems and questions. He is the face of the police apparatus that used to be highly anonymous. The police are the only government department accessible and available 24 hours a day, seven days a week. The family officer is to increase that accessibility and availability. When necessary, he can also guide the public through the labyrinth of police bureaucracy. He will try to solve the public's problems, but even more will try to teach the public how to solve their own problems. By encouraging them to solve their problems independently, self-confidence among the public will also grow.

The concept of community policing offers opportunities of turning the calculating citizen into a responsible citizen. Many members of the public would welcome a return to the social control of a few decades ago, but that is no longer possible. What does lie within our reach is that new networks will start to flourish and new social contacts will develop, that groups of citizens will start to feel responsible for their immediate surroundings again. When the public sees that they are surrounded by police officers showing involvement in their neighbourhood or district, this will create positive effects. When the public really feels a sense of partnership in relation to the problems in their neighbourhood, we have reached a great deal. Today, this is still possible; ten years from now some neighbourhoods might otherwise have become no-go areas for us.

One of the aspects of community policing, as we try to introduce it, is directed at schoolchildren. We have developed a so-called 'school adoption plan'. Crime prevention starts with children, first of all with those at primary schools. This school adoption plan, as the name indicates, implies that a police officer adopts a school. He regularly visits that school, stands in front of the class and gives information. He talks with the children, not like a Dutch uncle, but ready to listen. Thus, the police officer becomes a person with whom the children are acquainted, and after school hours they will meet him again in the street. In this way, a bond can grow between children and the police.

Another aspect of community policing is that new networks facilitate the gathering of all sorts of information, particularly criminal information. This process will only be reinforced by the ever-faster development of our communication technology. Radio communication and compact computer information equipment will enable us to have, so to speak, an office available at every street corner. By means of advanced, compact, mobile equipment it will soon be possible to receive, process and transmit information anywhere in the city. It is not science fiction to say that in a number of years the street officer will be equipped with what we call an information pistol. These developments will increase immensely the availability of the police for deployment. Community policing will also lead to responsibilities being allocated to the organisation's lowest possible level, and the current, highly hierarchical organisation model will become a thing of the past. This prospect for the future means that there will never be a consolidated police service. Police organisations should change constantly. New and higher demands will continue to be made on our professionalism. This is the daily challenge to each of us.

9. THE COMMUNAL POLICE MODEL IN HAJDÚ BIHAR COUNTY

S. Sutka

1. Introduction

The expression 'communal police' is met ever more frequently in specialist literature. For us the actuality of the topic was brought home by the change in regime, accompanied by a radical change in social and economic conditions. Because of these changes we had to reformulate our police and criminal investigation policy. We obviously had to maintain our reactive ability but we now also had to win the support of the public. Today it has become more clear to us than ever that the police can only work efficiently if they have the confidence and support of the population. Making the organisation receptive to cooperating with the social forces made numerous organisational changes necessary.

Here I wish to share some of our practical experiences. Thus you might find arguments and counter-arguments for strengthening or modifying your own concepts. Being fully aware of the fact that characteristic conditions prevail in police work for each country, I am convinced, however, that our profession has such general characteristics that knowledge about these characteristics will prove useful.

One of the results of the present IACP conference could therefore be that, following the discussions about the questions waiting to be solved regarding the police and police work, we could draft a course of action that takes into account fundamental communal trends as well as the increase in crime.

International trends and experiences offer new perspectives for the cooperation of police organisations. Knowledge of police working methods in the highly developed countries is extremely valuable to the Hajdú Bihar County Police.

After this introduction I would like to present a brief historical overview which reflects the fundamental problems, the social-political milieu, that influenced the police organisation in Hungary in general and that of Hajdú Bihar County in particular.

2. Historical overview

The former regime – which ruled for more than four decades – interlaced communal life at every level. The total dictatorship, the powerful state, felt and exercised the need to supervise everyday life. The decisions on criminal policy came from the top, the local apparatus was left solely with the role of implementation. As a result of this excessive centralisation, the police forces were withdrawn from the smaller communities. Police organisations with excessive numbers of staff were created. At the same time, because of the increase in municipal crime, police patrols were rarely dispatched to villages. Apart from the district officers, who also carried out a large part of investigative activities, other police personnel hardly ever appeared in the area. As a result, our connections with the citizens were formulated in a characteristic manner. The authoritarian attitude towards the population, discrimination, the supervision of those with different opinions, fostered bad feelings towards the police. A significant part of the inhabitants were reluctant to accept the police force, and looked down on its members. The contradictions were increased by the lack of legal regulations regarding police work, thus both secret and open activities functioned without any control.

The security strategy of the police in this period, and the criminal predictions based on a certain ideology, proved to be false. In the 1980s our police were caught in a vicious circle, which was reflected by a sustained rise in crime. The index of detected crimes, which had earlier stagnated at national level, first exceeded the 130,000 limit, then the 140,000 limit, and finally, by the end of the 1980s, this number even exceeded 200,000. The crime index of Hajdú Bihar County also reflected these countrywide trends.

The increase in crime, together with the alienation which resulted from municipal anonymity, had a stimulating effect on research into and development of the means of crime-prevention and operating methods of the police. It became clear that the demand for the investigation and detection of crimes, and the need for police presence in public areas, could no longer be brought into harmony with the needs of the community. At least not with the inflexible police organisation we had at our disposal. Therefore in 1989 it was decided that the police would have to be reorganised.

The characteristics mentioned above had as a result that our police were unprepared, both in structure as in working-methods, for the radical change in regime that occurred. The processes indicating the way of change accelerated in May 1990. Favourable social and political conditions necessary to create a police apparatus adjusted to the challenges of the time were created. The relationship between the sciences and police work also changed. Through the good offices of the TC TEAM CONSULT-Company, the force was subjected to a detailed situation analysis, the likes of which it had never experienced before. As a result of this thorough examination, new priorities were set. These were: our relationship with the public should be put on a new footing; more time should be invested in improving public security; policemen should adopt a new attitude; and a decentralised organisation should be established.

The establishment of local government accelerated this process. That is to say, local government, as the intermediary of the inhabitants' expectations and demands, took and continues to take measures to ensure that a police unit, which exceeds the district officers' system in both numbers and technical equipment, becomes operational in its area of administration. This was generally done in those areas where there used to be a traditional police presence, that is, where there used to be a gendarmerie post, a sub-police station or a guard room.

A strategy in accordance with social demands had to be developed, implying optimal service to the interests of a democratic society. This was taken as self-evident, for the crime rates in this period had soared to a level that we had never before experienced. This increase even started to endanger the new developments of social change. The situation worsened because the increase in the number of crimes committed was followed by a rearrangement in the types of crimes. Violent offences came to the fore, endangering the life and property of the population at large, committed in an organised manner and utilising international connections. At the same time a huge number of criminals appeared who made use of the boom in private enterprise and the slackening of the general situation.

3. The demographic picture and the criminal situation in Hajdú Bihar County

The social-economic environment of Hajdú Bihar County, in combination with its geographical regional position and demographic picture, has become the medium and creator of internal conflicts and tensions that put several symptoms, including crime, in a new light. The increase in crime took place in such a way that almost everything of value protected under criminal law was at risk. It can be concluded from criminal statistics that these symptoms did not prevail in the same way in other areas of Hungary. Hajdú Bihar County stood out as far as criminal intensity was concerned. It became one of the country's most infected areas. Regarding the number of crimes per 100,000 inhabitants, we are now solidly in the top quarter of the national ratings.

Hajdú Bihar County covers an area of 6,211 km². With regard to its size, it is the fourth largest county in the country. Its geographical position – close to Rumania and the Ukraine – clearly influences the criminal situation. This has a direct effect on the people living here, having a negative influence on their subjective sense of security. Worth mentioning here is the traffic checkpoint at Artand, in our area of operation, which deals with large numbers of passengers and freight, and all this mixed with a wide variety of criminal activities.

It is a characteristic of the region that it is rich in cultural and intellectual traditions. This stems from its history, the responsiveness towards social and intellectual progress, and from being directly involved in vital questions regarding Hungarian nationality, our national language and culture.

The city of Debrecen is dominant in our area of operation, being a seat of learning and East Hungary's educational and scientific centre. Tourism was always concentrated here and at Hajdúszoboszlo throughout the year. Tourism is one of the most important economic sectors of the county, providing a living for a significant proportion of the population. Therefore police attention in the field of tourism is among the special tasks of the Hajdú Bihar County Police.

Variety is characteristic of our county's communities. Besides widely spaced and sparsely populated communities, densely populated areas can also be found. There are 79 communities in our area of operations. Urban crime has become dominant in the regional structure of criminal offences. By Hungarian standards, the county town of Debrecen, from the perspective of criminality, has to be seen as a metropolis. Fifty per cent of the crimes detected in our area of responsibility are committed here, the indexes of which exceed some of the criminal statistics for the country as a whole.

Besides the economic data, the demographic-social composition of the population is of dominant importance from the perspective of crime assessment. According to the last population census, almost 550,000 people live in Hajdú Bihar County, which is 5.2% of the country's total population. In the make-up of nationalities we find a significant population of approximately 50,000 gypsies. Rumanians, Germans and other minority groups live in our region in much smaller numbers.

While examining the interrelations of crime, we cannot ignore those significant differences which can be recognised from the regional data on economic geography and criminal statistics. The changes not only affect the various social strata differently, but the various branches as well. It follows from this that the seriousness and magnitude of the social problems that arise are of a different nature in the various regions of the country.

Because of the reformation of the economic structure, we now also have to face the fact that unemployment appears to be conducive to crime, phenomenon that was incompatible with and almost unknown within the earlier political-economic system. These difficulties also test the psychic and physical endurance of the population. Unfortunately, this problem occurs in our county in a more serious way, because the so-called Eastern region is lagging behind in comparison with other regions of the country. Our economic structure can be labelled as agrarian-industrial. Because of the natural endowments, agriculture was always the occupation that provided a living for the inhabitants here. In this connection, a negative factor should be mentioned: the consequences of the privatisation of arable land must be listed as a side effect of the change of regime. Unsolved ownership relationships have almost disrupted this industry, thus increasing the problems of unemployment. At present the rate of unemployment in our county is 16%, which is 4 to 5% higher compared with the national average. For the gypsy population, the unemployment rates are far worse: 85 to 87% of them are unemployed. So their situation may easily be described as desperate. As a result of this, those forms of criminal offences occur which we call 'bread-and-butter crimes'. The handling and processing of petty crime, mainly against property, presents a great test of strength, not only of the police organisation, but also of the population.

The general feeling is influenced more and more by the fact that the safety of the property of the inhabitants has been under severe pressure. The crimes committed against personal belongings have soared. The proportion of offences against property, within the total number of crimes, is close to 75%. A significant role is played here by burglary, which has become one of the more professional criminal occupations. It should also be mentioned that the crimes in connection with stolen vehicles have risen drastically in recent years. Second only to Budapest, crimes of this type are committed in the greatest number in Debrecen and its surroundings.

These crimes are committed in an organised way and because of the proximity of borders, their international character is increasing.

Among crimes of a disorderly nature, the public is most irritated by the spread of robbery. The majority of robberies occur in public areas, and are characterised by the drastic hold-up method, and the threat of gas or fire-arms, or imitations.

With the reforms towards a market economy, financial or 'white-collar' crimes have also increased rapidly. The trends display a varied picture. Among the most frequently committed financial crimes, fraud, smuggling, counterfeiting of currency, and cases of breaching foreign exchange-regulations should be mentioned.

The change of regime not only means a change of organisations, legal regulations, management models and the like, but also the modification of consciousness. In accordance with this, the image of our police force has been reformulated in recent years. Our duty has been redefined as protecting the whole community and human values. The citizen-friendly, efficient police force does not confront the community, but cooperates with it and enjoys its trust. This is illustrated by our 'We serve and protect' slogan, which fundamentally tries to establish a model for a serving police force which is close to the public. It is an essential requirement for the management of our police force as regards staff and personnel that these specific expectations should be taken into account in the course of performing their duties. Still, in spite of this, prejudices and fixed ideas that are the result of past experiences still exist. Emotional motives change more slowly than the actual situation. We know very well that we will only be capable of changing this situation by purposeful and hard work.

Nevertheless, the results of the changes are already visible. The contradictions of the social and economic changes, and the reliance of the criminal investigation organisations and the community on each other, have actually resulted in the public and the police getting closer to each other. The population has accepted the fact that the police force, as an organisation, performs a basic function indispensable to the state, an essential part of the state's system of organisations. The attitude of the public towards the police has changed, based on two expectations: on the one hand the public wants the police force to become democratic, to strengthen its serving function, and to be considerate with regard to the population. On the other hand, the public wants the police to be resolute in maintaining legal guarantees, to ensure public order and security under all circumstances.

4. The development of an organisational model in accordance with the expectations of the community.

The demands of the power of the state (parliament, government) are expressed in laws and other legal regulations. Centrally drafted requirements that affect the population as a whole are enforced through legal implementation of state administration. The requirements of local government are formulated in accordance with the needs of the communities. The legal basis for these is found partly in the law relating to the police and partly in the law relating to local government.

The structural organisation and operating methods of the Hajdú Bihar County Central Police, have been developed according to social requirements drafted within the context of legal regulations. The requirements of a constitutional state demand the establishment of a more open, modern police force, with better support from the community. Party-neutrality, independence and subordination to the law are key words in this respect.

In connection with the modernisation of the organisation, emphasis was put on a bottom-up development and the installation of a modern police network in the front line. This is to be understood in two ways. Firstly, the structure and positions of sub units of the central police office was affected, and secondly the spatial arrangement of actual daily duties. As regards the organisational structure, it is worth mentioning the district officers and district officer groups (2–3 persons) close to the inhabitants, together with the newly created guardrooms (7–24 persons) and police stations (52-65 persons). In the operating area of the Hajdú Bihar County Central Police, 8 police stations and 12 guardrooms subordinate to these are in operation at present, totalling about 1,500 officers and civil servants.

The demands put on our police force are summarised in the Law on the Police. On the basis of this our duties can be divided into three main groups. The first is maintaining law and order, the second is the carrying out of duties in connection with criminal law, while the third is state administration work.

While maintaining law and order, we pay special attention to a constant police presence in public areas, together with the development of a suitable ability to react. With all of this, in addition to a better prevention and detection of crimes, we wish to improve the population's sense of security. At the majority of police offices outside the county seat, the preventive and reactive activities are not separated in providing public services. In practice, this means that it depends on the operative situation of public security as to whether prevention or a reactive police presence is required. On the basis of conclusions drawn from analytical and evaluative activities, periodic concentrations of forces are carried out. The object of this, beyond a demonstrative police presence, is a thorough police inspection of local areas, and the carrying out of checks and searches in those areas where this is demanded by the public.

The trends of crime in densely populated areas and the maintenance of law and order required an entirely new method of operation to be developed which would adjust adequately to these changed conditions.

An important question in our public security strategy was how we could react quickly to events requiring action. Therefore, in 1994 we established a so-called Action Control Centre at the Debrecen Police Office. We were the first in Hungary. The essence of our concept for structural modernisation was that, with expedient re-grouping of existing staff and technical implements, we aimed at the integration of the various service branches – public security, crime – into one organisation. We determined the function of the Action Control Centre to be an immediate and expedient reaction to events, and its structure was developed according to this. This professional integration increased the complex nature of police measures, and the higher degree of district management presence favourably affected the level of work, which was acknowledged by the public.

Among the sub-organisations of the police office, it is worth mentioning the four relatively independent guardrooms. These units direct their public law and order maintenance personnel into public areas, concentrating on established areas of operation. With the so-called classic provision of public service, we had the opportunity to establish closer contact with the population, and to broaden our existing connections. A further advantage was experienced by the creation of police stations. Through these, it became possible to make those directly responsible for the area accountable for their actions, and within these units the strengthening of a collective spirit was favourably influenced because fewer staff were present.

Our connections with the public were put on a new footing in the area of public security service activities. Here one should think mainly of the duties for security at sporting events, during which dialogues were initiated with hard-core supporters. As a result of this, events requiring police intervention at matches now hardly ever occur.

In our judgment, the formulation of traffic safety also forms an integral part of public order. The changes in objective and subjective conditions determining road safety, together with the status of personnel and equipment at the Central Police Office, stimulated us into re-structuring the traffic service organisation.

The activity of the accident prevention section, situated within the county department organisation, is noteworthy in this respect. They carry out continuous propaganda work at various events, in the interests of preventing accidents. With their accident prevention activities they aim at the age-group most affected and endangered in traffic.

Today, the 24-hour non-stop competitions announced for university and college students can already be said to be traditional. With their varied programmes they have aroused the interest of the youth. An important question for the police is of the impression that is obtained and the sort of value systems formed in the growing intellectual strata regarding the work of the police and the force itself.

The specialist criminal area has also altered significantly. We have established a crime prevention service, with a basic function of maintaining connections with the population and the participating social organisations. Our established crime prevention programme seeks answers to the real challenges of crime, characteristic for our area. The DADA programme, introduced on the basis of the American DARE example, mainly offers help to the endangered young age groups in acknowledging, handling and preventing problems of smoking, drugs and AIDS. 'The neighbours for each other' movement was similarly taken up by our crime prevention service, which in its objectives, among others, is oriented towards reducing the indifference of the population to each other, and a reduction of the opportunities for crime.

Proof of our readiness for cooperation with the population can be found in the fact that, while keeping in mind legal regulations, the County Chief of Police and the eight Police Constables provide information and make reports. Beyond this, we try to engage in continuous dialogue and exchange of ideas with the mayors and local governmental bodies. This means that, at regular intervals, consultations are held with the mayors on the actual problems of crime and crime prevention. On these occasions, the competent police chiefs provide information to the mayors, and make suggestions on trends. Although they fall outside the police's competence with regard to criminal and crime prevention activities, they nevertheless can be influenced by measures taken by local government. Generally these discussions take place at the meetings of the public security and crime prevention committees operating under local governments, the establishment of which is provided for in the Law on the Police. Significant social relations are also established with local inhabitants, an opportunity that is realised in the so-called civilian forums and on police chiefs' consulting days.

Cooperation with the home-guard units should be seen as an extremely important way of maintaining contact with the population. The observational, patrolling and indicating activities of these social self-protection groups can contribute to the improvement of public order and the security of the individual communities. At present 49 home-guard units operate in Hajdú Bihar County, with a membership of 2,000 citizens. On one hand, the large number of participants expresses the demands of the community, and on the other favourably influences the image of the police. The establishment of the Information Office operating in Debrecen has also positively influenced our relationship with the inhabitants. Here, advisory services are carried out in connection with crime prevention.

The media play a dominant role in the allocation of communal requirements. This role is performed in part by the journalists, who record events accurately in writing and photographs. Publicised opinions also contribute by significantly influencing the image formed of the work of the police. As a shadow over the majority of correct public information, stories are published that undermine the people's sense of security in connection with public law and order. Knowledge of this guides us in our efforts towards and continuous, open cooperation with the representatives of the press.

5. Our objectives

Among our short-term conceptions, priority is given to ensuring customary patterns of life in public areas by police methods, within the boundaries of legal regulations. In the interests of this, the planning, organisation and execution of public area service, with the full-scale utilisation of the available forces and implements, is directed towards crime prevention. To this end, and beyond the daily service, use is made of those demonstrative implements which serve to discourage those persons inclined towards crime against public property.

Together with this, we wish to further maintain police activity at a high level. This activity must make clear that, in the interests of protecting the law-abiding citizen, the police will take aggressive measures against those who wish to take advantage by disregarding the rightful interests of others.

We are continually seeking opportunities to modernise the professionalism of the criminal investigation service and uniformed public security service of the police, to bring them closer to the people, and adjust them to the challenges of life. In connection with this, we wish in future, while handling so-called mass-cases, to increase the number of deputy detective officers.

The growing connection of Hungary with the European integration processes, and the strengthening of the international nature of crime, both make it necessary to regard the development of our police force's international connections as a task of great importance. One of the important objectives in this area could be a better utilisation by the police of the opportunities hidden in the existing cooperation between internationally operating criminal organisations.

10. THE ORGANISATIONAL CRIME MONEY-LAUNDERING CYCLE IN ITALIAN SAUCE

E.U. Savona

1. Introduction

Focusing on the Italian situation, this contribution deals with what is defined as the organised crime money-laundering cycle, that is the connection between the ways organised criminals produce their criminal proceeds and the ways they launder them in order to conceal their criminal origin. Attacking this cycle is becoming more important than attacking the individual activities carried out by the criminals. The content of economic and organised crime is becoming less differentiated because the interdependence between the different forms of organisational crimes such as fraud, money-laundering and corruption is growing in complexity and professionalism. In this process, money-laundering is the end of the tunnel that criminal organisations run through in order to legitimise themselves and invest their proceeds.

Analysing the main organised groups operating in Italy in the second paragraph, this paper considers the variety of their organised activities either in the illegal markets or as infiltration into the legitimate industries. The third paragraph deals with the different measures used to combat money-laundering activities, and the fourth paragraph discusses some of the main trends that characterise the organised crime money-laundering cycle in the European Union countries.

2. Confrontation with competition and emerging difficulties

2.1. THE ITALIAN MAFIA

The Mafia has been variously defined. In Italy, the term generally refers to the Sicilian Mafia or Cosa Nostra, the Neapolitan Camorra, the Calabrian 'Ndrangheta, and the Sacra Corona Unita in Apulia. The most important of these is clearly the Cosa Nostra.

In 1990, the total amount of money produced by Italian criminals was estimated by the Italian Central Institute for Statistics at between approximately 21.5 and 24 billion dollars. At least 50% of this amount can be attributed to organised crime. The Sicilian Mafia's share is estimated as being between one third and one half of this amount.

Although many of the activities conducted by the Cosa Nostra are still regional and its power remains based in Southern Italy, Cosa Nostra has increasingly become a transnational enterprise. This has been facilitated by migration flows.

Italian criminal organisations, however, have recently suffered a number of setbacks. Their chances of survival in the future depend on a set of new factors:

- the Mafia assaults on the Italian judicial authorities between 1983 and 1992 ultimately proved counterproductive. Its inter-linking with political power and the establishment of a collusive relationship with the state has also come under increasing attack;

- these criminal organisations are also faced with the new threat of the "pentiti" (supergrasses): criminals from organisations deciding to collaborate with the judges, helping them to uncover the structure and the activities of the organisation in exchange for a reduced sentence;

- the opening of frontiers and of markets which offer, on the one hand, new opportunities for criminal activities and, on the other hand, new competition or collaboration among criminal groups from other countries.

Although in recent years in Italy the Mafia has been weakened by the upsurge of popular sentiment against it and by the relevant changes in the political situation, criminal organisations remain a major challenge to the law enforcement authorities. All the traditional criminal groups in Italy are, at present, re-organising their structures and activities as a result of the reasons just cited. Cosa Nostra, for example, in order to protect itself against the revelations of the supergrasses, is creating a new generation of 'mafiosi'. The Mafia is abandoning its traditional code of rules, it is changing its structure and it is turning into an organisation made up of secret cells. Each of these cells has its specific tasks and role within the overall organisations, the members of one cell knowing nothing about the other cells. Also, increasing use is made of common criminals. Next to this, the internal structure of Cosa Nostra has changed radically. It has become even more closed, articulated into watertight compartments, impermeable to investigations.

Italian criminal organisations are trying to win positions within the international market while simultaneously maintaining control over the territory and their criminal and commercial activities. They are seeking to do so by becoming more sophisticated and more professional in managing investments, and in differentiating them among a wide range of activities. Accordingly, the four main Italian criminal organisations, in order to reduce the risk of conflicts and competition among themselves and to coordinate control over the territory and interactions with foreign criminal groups, have specialised in certain fields, and are operating side by side in several sectors.

2.2. ORGANISED CRIME AND BUSINESS CRIME

As regards the criminal activities of the Italian Mafia, two aspects should be borne in mind when evaluating criminal business decisions: an even finer distinction between criminal activities and organised business crime activities. Business in prohibited goods no longer seems to be the most profitable one. The Italian police authorities report that the Mafia is investing huge resources in the trade of protected, damaged, low quality goods or out of date products and counterfeits. This major new activity stems from several factors: the personal and criminal contacts the Mafia has built in the Eastern European countries in recent years, and the Mafia communities directly established there; investments in these areas in structures and in institutional and political contacts (bribery). Criminal organisations act as intermediary agencies for enterprises in their regions, supplying them with contacts. This role helps criminal organisations to strengthen their influence on the territory. They also offer the enterprises consultancy on tax evasion, fiscal fraud and export tax fraud.

An example of organised business criminal activity which has been rapidly converted to new criminal purposes is fraud against the European Union (EU). Since 1 January 1993, the expiry date for customs barriers, criminals have increasingly utilised their capabilities in the commission of VAT fraud. The mechanism is simple, and exploits weak transitional legislation (in force until 31 December 1996) which allows payment of VAT according to the amount declared by the buyer, not according to customs controls at the border. It turns out that a third of all EU frauds are committed in Italy. In monetary terms, the balance is even worse: 67% of the total sum is defrauded in Italy (79.49 million ECU).

71

The building sector has always been a privileged one where activities of organised crime in Italy are concerned, because it does not require high technology or expertise. It can be used as a money-laundering mechanism (through the payment of salaries, purchase of machinery and materials), and it is of considerable use in the control of the criminals' territory by providing work opportunities and channelling political consensus. There is in fact a connection among Camorra organisations; political power and public administration and the different economic sectors based on a convergence of interests. The politician assigns works to the entrepreneur in exchange for a bribe; the entrepreneur pays bribes to the politician and gives money and work to the mafioso; the mafioso in turn takes money from the entrepreneur, assures social peace and control of the workforce, and grants political support to the politician who started the chain. To control the building sector, organised crime has invested in gaining the monopoly in the key sectors of soil transportation, the supply of building materials, the production and distribution of concrete and cement. The Italian political crisis since 1990 was soon followed by the crisis in the building sector, the most corrupt sector. Therefore, this huge source of proceeds has been stopped temporarily.

Ten years ago, the waste disposal sector was a marginal component of the range of activities run by the Camorra. Around 1988, matters began to change. Criminal clans realised the importance of waste disposal as an illegal business and moved into the sector, creating a network of fictitious companies: devices through which to channel bribes to the political parties. Also the Sacra Corona Unita has entered the waste business, collaborating when necessary with the Cosa Nostra, the Cammorra and the 'Ndrangheta.

2.3. COOPERATION WITH FOREIGN CRIMINAL ORGANISATIONS

Another new and profitable activity is counterfeiting. Here too, direct links have been established with foreign criminal organisations, especially the Russian Mafia. The forging of documents is an activity which can be both profitable and suitable for a wide range of purposes: false papers for illegal immigrants, false bank documents, such as certificates, bonds, means of payment, and recently also US dollar banknotes. In fact, in Russia the most widely used currency is not the rouble, but the dollar. In exchange for forged dollars, the Italian organisations receive arms, chemicals for drug production and raw materials to sell on legal markets. The production of counterfeit goods, brands and fashion items, which are then exported to the new and profitable markets in the Eastern Countries, is also worth mentioning here. These goods are produced locally in Italy using immigrant black labour, or they are imported from Asian countries and then assembled in Italy or simply marked by the Italian organisations.

Despite the profitability of these other sectors, the drugs trade is still of crucial importance. In 1994, 'ecstasy' replaced heroin in the international markets. Cocaine, however, moved into top position as the most widely smuggled drug from Latin America to Europe, overtaking heroin, which had predominated since 1985. Nevertheless, the most important increase in drugs trafficking has been registered in the synthetic drugs trade.

Turning to cocaine trafficking: 'Operation Cartagine' (which began on March 5 and ended on March 22, 1995) has revealed that the business is monopolised by a well-structured Mafia organisation ('Ndrangheta in this specific case), working in collaboration with the Colombian cartels, and with the Italo-American Caruana family as a very important link between them. The 'Ndrangheta is believed to purchase and sell a huge amount of cocaine throughout the entire country, without competition from other criminal organisations. It operates at the same hierarchical level and with the full cooperation of the Colombians (law enforcement officials say that 'Ndrangheta men occupy leading positions in the Colombian cartels).

The Colombian organisations in Italy are the most efficient. They are the most up-to-date in terms of technology and communication instruments. They also use experts and research groups of experts and lawyers, who are paid to conduct feasibility studies, sector investment programmes, to examine law enforcement activities and to evaluate the profitability of any new licit or illicit activity. With this expertise available, the Colombians are highly dynamic and competitive: ready to exploit new market opportunities or geographical areas.

There is scant information on the Russian criminal organisations active in Italy. Their main characteristics seem to be a lack of financial experience combined with an impressive amount of cash and financial resources. According to what little information is available, these organisations have been mainly active in the purchase of luxury goods, but also in the trafficking of counterfeit dollars, arms and migrants (especially prostitutes), working in close collaboration with the Italian criminal organisations.

As far as other foreign criminal organisations in Italy are concerned, these tend to assume forms of traditional roots similar to those adopted by Italians forty years ago when they emigrated throughout the world. Strong ethnic identification, solidarity and *omertà*, cultural barriers such as dialect which make these organisations impenetrable to police. For example, there is hardly any information available on the Chinese Triads or other

Asian criminal organisations operating in Italy. The only thing the Italian police know is that Triads usually utilise front activities such as restaurants to cover trafficking in illegal aliens. Chinese organisations such as the 'Green Dragon' are known to be especially active in the transportation of Chinese illegal immigrants from the natural harbours in Apulia to the bigger cities.

The problem of clandestine migration is a particularly severe one in Italy, because of its geographical position, because of its lack of legislation and regulations on the matter, and, as a consequence, because of the country's few and inefficient border controls. In fact, due to bureaucratic and political delays, Italy has been forced to postpone its entry into the European area of the free circulation of persons envisaged by the Schengen Convention of 14 July 1985. There is clear evidence that clandestine immigration still continues. This activity is particularly remunerative and is controlled by criminal organisations, both Italian and foreign. An example is provided by the large numbers of migrants of different origins (from Albania, China, Pakistan and Kurdistan) sailing from the Albanian coast. These migrants cross the Adriatic in small boats and disembark on the Italian coast.

Worth mentioning is the kidnapping activity on the Isle of Sardinia that began once more in 1995: 9 kidnappings in 1993, 4 in 1994 and 2 until May 1995. It seems that the problem of laundering and reinvestment of the proceeds of ransom demands is solved. They exchange the ransom money for drugs, making this exchange with major national organised criminal groups which have gained expertise or have good contacts with professionals in this field.

3. Responding to the money-laundering cycle

3.1. THE ROLE OF FINANCIAL INSTITUTIONS

Notwithstanding an efficient legislation which makes the financial market one of the most closely monitored and transparent ones in Europe, Italian financial institutions and banks seem unable (or unwilling) to resist efforts by organised crime to use them to launder their illicit proceeds. This has been clearly shown by the Italian police operation 'Dinero', which began in November 1993 and ended in March 1994. A professional legally tried to acquire a small-sized bank in a remote Italian region. This bank was operating in the agricultural sector, and would have been the first of a network of laundering institutions. It came under control of this professional without the use of violent methods, but through a huge influx of capital from a shareholder without direct or apparent links with criminal organisations. The unusually high amount of transactions and specific operations, compared with the usual business of other local banks, should have provoked suspicion of involvement with money-laundering practices. This suspicion, however, was not caused by unusual transactions, but arose after another investigation of the individual had begun. At the end of September, another case was uncovered by the Italian police. A bank was found to be owned by Cosa Nostra bosses, and run by a professional with good contacts within public institutions and the licit economic sector. The bank had been operating since 1960, and had laundered illicit money for the Cosa Nostra families.

Although not directly controlled by criminal organisations, financial institutions seem rather unwilling to cooperate with the police or the judicial authorities, at least until investigations show evidence of financial operations to back illicit activities. The legal requirement to denounce suspicious operations has not become standard practice, because of the suspected complicity of bank employees, because transactions were previously commingled in foreign banks, and because the business activities of a front company are difficult to identify as concealing criminal activities.

3.2. NEW INVESTMENT STRATEGIES OF THE MAFIA

Over the last two decades, the money-laundering activities of Italian criminal organisations have grown increasingly sophisticated. They aim in particular at gaining control over non-financial institutions in order to avoid the law regulating the financial sector, and to avoid the wide range of movement techniques carried out in financial institutions.

Police investigations also report that traditional markets (cattle raising, and slaughtering) are subject to money-laundering activities. This traditional sector is well known by the criminal groups because it is part of the economic life in their territory, and cash transactions are still widely used and accepted.

The new investment strategies of Italian organised criminal groups reveal the increasing sophistication of the Mafia. These strategies consist in the first place of the acquisition of control over specific economic activities in specific areas of the country. The most recent data on these activities show that the building trade is the sector most tightly penetrated. This sector has always been the most conducive for criminal organisations because of a low level of technology and a considerable amount of initial capital investment. Overall it is one of the most profitable of the licit activities because of the availability of public works contracts. These latter

constitute the Mafia's natural link with the political parties: criminal organisations pay bribes to political parties and ensure politicians their support by exerting more or less violent control over local electors. Illicit investment strategies also concern commercial and artisan enterprises, the
real estate market and restaurants, supermarkets, car dealerships, travel
agencies, hotels, and shops of different kinds. The investment of illicit
proceeds serves several purposes: laundering illicit proceeds, covering
forms of illicit trafficking and controlling the territory and its economic
sectors. In the second place, they consist of intervention through usury in
economic sectors affected by recession. The widespread phenomenon of
usury stems from two main factors: the economic crisis that has affected
Italy for the last few years, and the inefficiency or complicity of the Italian
banking system – and hence the difficulty of small firms in obtaining
credit from legal financial instructions. These two conditions force the
owners of small businesses to resort to usury networks. They obtain credit
at a higher interest rate, thus increasing their financial difficulties until
they are forced to close down or to sell the business. Criminal organisations force the owners to repay the loan or to sell the business to them at a
very low price. The owner can also be used as a front-man or intermediary. Usury is a widespread activity which is constantly on the increase.

Geographically speaking, the investments of the Mafia are not limited
to the Southern part of the country, but increasing evidence shows that
even the industrialised North is affected by Mafia capital. There is evidence of several suspect property transferrals of restaurants, houses, bars,
hotels, and in the entertainment industry.

Some organisations tend to develop inner financial task forces and to
specialise in this activity, selling the service to other criminal organisations. In fact, money-laundering is a risky and thus very costly service
which must be used to reinvest illegal proceeds, but it increasingly proves
to be lucrative. Other Italian criminal organisations prefer to use external
launderers, who have traditionally served criminals, politicians or tax
evaders to export their bribes or illicit earnings abroad, or to invest them.

The police operation 'Unigold' found that some of the leading firms in
the Italian gold and jewellery sector were acting as accomplices to the
Colombian cartels in selling large amounts of gold to their branches in
Panama. The gold was sold in Panama and the money then returned to
Colombia. These operations are the most striking evidence that the traditional organisations have renewed their capabilities, acquiring financial
and business expertise in order to protect their earnings against detection
by the police.

Money-laundering methods range from the most sophisticated methods to the simplest ones; activities such as the 'spalloni' (criminals who cross the border with bags full of money), or throwing bags of money over the border, or the transhipment of money in cargoes or in trucks. All these activities are flourishing among criminal organisations in an attempt to diversify their efforts. Sometimes commercial and industrial activities are used only as fronts, to physically ship money abroad: the police have reported several attempts to utilise Italian furniture shipped world-wide as containers full of notes. Fronts are used also for conversion techniques carried out at international level such as, for example, the sale or export of assets (often with false import or export invoices), real estate, precious metals or goods.

4. Organised crime in a European sauce

4.1. GLOBALISATION: NEW OPPORTUNITIES FOR ORGANISED CRIME

The internal situation of the countries of the European Union is characterised by the relevant and stable presence of Italian organised criminal groups and by the development of 'domestic bilateral organisations' operating from country to country.

The European Union is also the crossroads of other criminal groups operating internationally, such as Nigerian groups (drug-trafficking), groups from the Maghreb area (hashish) and East Asian groups. From the Middle East, Turkish and Pakistani groups control the trafficking of heroin from the Middle East and Central Asia. The threat of the progressive expansion of organised groups from Eastern and Central Europe is common knowledge. From South America, Colombian cartels are still predominant in the importation of cocaine, helped by national criminal groups. Galicians in Spain and Mafia in Italy cooperate with these cartels to import and distribute cocaine in the whole of Europe.

The analysis carried out by TRANSCRIME (University of Trento) shows the progressive multiplication towards Europe and the ramification from European key points of trafficking routes either by sea, air or land.

The entry of Eastern organised crime in the international market has changed and increased the routes traditionally used. Russia and the other Eastern European regions are increasingly becoming the new transit routes for drugs trafficking, as well as for other criminal purposes (e.g. the smuggling of illegal aliens, stolen cars).

Since the crime industry is about the criminal exploitation of business opportunities and is dominated by supply organisations, it is not surprising that we have seen the development of organisations that transport illicit commodities across national jurisdictions. With the globalisation of trade and of consumer demand for leisure products, it is only natural that criminal organisations should move from the level of national activity to that of transnational operations. Just as new opportunities have opened up for legitimate entrepreneurs, opportunities for illicit enterprise have increased too. There are several activities that transnational criminal organisations typically engage in that deserve further attention.

4.2. MAJOR CRIMINAL ACTIVITIES

It has already been outlined that drug-trafficking, being a very profitable industry, still remains the major source of income for most criminal organisations operating in Europe.

Car theft has in the meantime also become an extensive problem in the European Union where the number of stolen cars almost tripled between 1989 and 1993. Based on the first national crime statistics for 1993 it can be estimated that some 250,000 passenger cars disappeared without trace in the EU last year. In certain cases, the cooperation of criminal syndicates with the military is of special importance. Until recently, the principal military air transportation centre was situated on Polish soil. Thieves steal cars in Germany and drive them to Poland. Then the cars are put on board military transportation and flown to Russian military airports. Russian companies which run the business are not necessarily part of the criminal ring, and sometimes they are even unaware (or prefer to be unaware) of the real origin of the cars, though, of course, the majority at least guesses where the cars come from.

Since 1988 the counterfeit industry has considerably increased the sophistication of its products and, in some instances, counterfeit credit cards are of better quality than the genuine cards they purport to be. In addition to counterfeit currency, bonds and other monetary instruments, there has been an escalation in the international production and fraudulent use of counterfeit access devices: commercial credit cards, telecommunications, computers, identification documents. The number of cases of counterfeit currency in Western Europe seems to have tripled in 1993 compared with 1991. Counterfeit money is becoming big business in Eastern Europe. The bleak economic outlook coupled with an unstable currency and high rate of inflation have led to the Deutschmark and the US dollar being used in place of the local currency in several CIS states, where even basic products can only be obtained with foreign currency. Such a situation provides ideal conditions for the production and distribution of counterfeit money.

Fraud with European Union funds is a traditional source of illicit proceeds, through the exploitation of inadequate legislation or by use being made of the lack of domestic controls. These criminal activities are not only carried out by professionals in legitimate industry at the margin of their business, but also by extensive organised criminal networks. They intertwine with normal trade and industry, and they use their facilities to sell products and to launder profits. Fraud occurs at different stages of the criminal process. Instruments such as front companies could either generate illegal proceeds from fraud, or they could be used to launder proceeds from other crimes, such as corruption. The number of frauds against the financial interests of the European Union is increasing. Data recently produced by the Commission of the European Community show the dimension of the phenomenon, and calls for more attention to be paid to the problem linked with international frauds, international organised crime and money-laundering. This criminal phenomenon involves goods of every kind through a wide range of more or less sophisticated methods. Other kinds of fraud, carried out by the same organisations, are VAT fraud and generally a wide range of financial and commercial frauds.

Criminal organisations are engaged in the massive smuggling of illegal aliens into the European Union from poor regions such as North Africa, Eastern Europe, Asia and South East Asia. The Russian Mafia group that controls certain routes makes an estimated $12 million a year on human traffic (people mainly coming from India, Pakistan, Somalia and Nigeria). The southern route is plied mainly by Romanian, Bulgarian, Turkish and former Yugoslavian citizens. Most of them arrive legally in Poland, taking advantage of an international agreement on visa-free tourist traffic. In Poland, the government estimates there are 100,000 migrants waiting to be smuggled into Germany. Smugglers are diversifying their routes: the landing places chosen are also Mediterranean ports, such as Marseilles and the coastal border in Italy. The head of the International Centre for Migration Policy Development in Vienna estimates that 300,000 people are smuggled into Western Europe every year, in comparison with the 2 million who got in legally in 1993. Not only does this once again threaten a basic ingredient of national sovereignty, it also places the immigrants themselves in jeopardy. These would-be immigrants are highly vulnerable, and women in particular are often forced into sexual slavery in order to pay off their debts to the criminal smuggling organisations. In fact, the increase in the smuggling of aliens is closely connected with prostitution.

Experts estimate that more than 10,000 young women have been recruited in East European countries.

In the former Soviet Union, considerable alarm has been created by the trafficking of nuclear materials. Because of an effective lack of demand, the danger arises that the organisations responsible may change tactics. If purchasers cannot be found and the material is in hand, extortion may appear particularly attractive. Moreover, as nuclear disarmament continues, the availability of material is likely to increase rather than decrease. Regardless of the question as to whether there are really any buyers, what is worrying is that organisations in Russia seem capable of operating at kilogram levels. There are currently several hundred tons of weapon-usable fissile material under inadequate physical security and material control in Russia. Kilogram quantities of weapon-grade fissile materials have been stolen from institutes in Russia since the break-up of the Soviet Union. The quantities stolen are sufficient to make small nuclear weapons. It is reasonable to conclude that sufficient fissile material can be diverted from Russian stockpiles with a high probability of success to provide a subnational group with one or two nuclear weapons, or even a rogue state with a sizeable arsenal.

4.3. INFILTRATION OF THE LEGAL ECONOMY

There is clear evidence emerging from cases in almost all the EU countries that criminals exert a more or less dangerous influence also within legal markets. Infiltration by organised crime groups, both traditional and relatively new ones, into the legitimate economy stems mainly from the need to invest their illicit proceeds in order to obtain a legitimate income, but also to reduce the overall risk of being detected and having their capital seized.

Recent stringent anti-money-laundering policies adopted by the member states have stimulated, via the money trail, a more efficient detection of the real owners of these proceeds, and the seizure of capital of illicit origin. It is therefore likely that organised criminals are seeking to internationalise themselves in order to reduce the risk that their criminal proceeds will be seized.

Infiltration of the licit economy also stems from another need: the history of criminal organisations throughout the world shows that they must constantly legitimise themselves in order to infiltrate the licit economy, to win an area of respectability, and thus enable their capital to circulate, thereby concealing any trace of its illicit origin. The legitimisation of their financial resources becomes the legitimisation of themselves. In the former Soviet Union, today's criminal classes might thus become tomorrow's ruling classes. In the history of criminal organisations there is always a stage at which they enter the legitimate economy. This seems to be happening in the European Union as well, due to its central geo-political and economic position. Analysis is therefore necessary of the effects exerted by the entrance of criminal organisations into the legitimate economy.

It is possible to distinguish three different effects and four areas of the legitimate economy in which they operate: the product market, the labour market, the capital market and, as a consequence, the stock market.

In the product market, the criminal enterprise can seriously distort competition between legal enterprises. This means that criminal organisations, in a context of different and varying relations, seek to acquire a leading position in the market, using the weapon of violence and breaches of the competition rules. It is possible today to observe in the European Union criminal organisations operating where profits are to be made, but also where the state or its institutions are weak. Moreover, also criminal penetration within the former Soviet republics is due to these two fundamental requisites: the maximisation of profits and the weakness of legislation and control instruments.

Another important factor is the distortions of the labour market. Two basic distortions arise in the labour market due to criminal infiltration: the first is that the criminal enterprise offers job opportunities at higher prices and with lower costs than those fixed in the legal market. Control is exerted over the workforce by the use of the threat of violence. By recruiting labour (especially foreign illicit aliens), criminal organisations directly handle job placements, negotiations, wages, thus protecting themselves against strikes or forms of claimant behaviour.

The capital market is also of major importance for criminal organisations. Almost all the EU authorities are aware of illicit capital entering capital markets. Increasingly, use is made of professionals and lawyers who make it possible to conceal the real ownership of money, thus averting the risk of its detection and seizure. It is evident that financial markets are the most desirable sectors for criminal infiltration. But there is a further aspect of penetration that is of particular importance: the effects on the stock market. Today, an interesting phenomenon within the European Union is that criminal organisations tend to invest laundered money by acquiring the property of enterprises. Through the acquisition of a limited corporation, the criminal investor can gain personal legitimisation, as well as a profitable, seemingly legitimate way to commingle licit and illicit funds, without directly using financial institutions.

4.4. FUTURE DEVELOPMENTS

New opportunities offered by the globalisation of markets seem to induce criminal organisations to develop in two different directions.

One is a development towards specialisation in one or more markets or in specific illicit goods. Increased competition between criminal organisations and investigations by law enforcement agencies are forcing criminal organisations to become increasingly efficient in their activities.

The other development is one of engaging in collateral activities because of their greater profitability, or because of the emergence of new needs. In this case, services or goods are provided on a free market basis: they are sold to other criminal organisations even though they may be competitors in a specific market or territory (arms trafficking and human smuggling, for example).

Not only organised criminal groups with common ethnic characteristics operate with a disciplined structure on these criminal markets, but also indigenous criminals, corrupt officials and dishonest entrepreneurs with international contacts. The latter form temporary networks for a specific purpose, upon completion of which they break up, or, at the same time, they involve other groups for other purposes not linked to the former.

This free environment, called the European Union, and the external variables described above seem to cause two major changes within the structure of criminal organisations. These changes move in two different directions. One being 'executive distancing', the other 'flexible networking'. The first change relates to the hierarchical distance between the leaders of a criminal enterprise and the rank-and-file, which is becoming increasingly greater. This means that the trail of evidence linking the crime and the top level has become obscured, providing insulation against law enforcement. At the lower levels, work is carried out by small units ('cells') which are aware of only a part of the organisation's activities, or which function only as serving units.

The second change reflects the need of criminal organisations to have a flexible structure in order to re-organise their activities swiftly, according to demand and to the number of competitors. Occasional business or specific targets increasingly require small task forces of criminally specialised experts who work with external individuals providing services and expertise that are unknown or not directly accessible to the criminal organisation.

4.5. COLLUSIVE AGREEMENTS

The organised groups analysed above, in order to commit the crimes outlined, require a wide range of services, information and capabilities. Therefore, an outlaw organisation cannot operate without close links with institutions, controlling authorities or other criminal groups.

Recently, attention has been paid at political and law-enforcement levels to the problem of collusive agreements among criminal groups. Recent alarm about such agreements denotes the awareness that the level of competition among criminal groups in some markets and its developments in some cases towards monopolistic positions or collusive agreements, is relevant for gaining understanding of the way in which organised crime faces opportunities and risks. Since collusive agreements are a better lever for optimisation, trading lesser opportunities against lesser risks in comparison with a monopoly where opportunities and risk are high, it is understandable that law enforcement agencies are concerned when a trend towards more collusive agreements develops. For the same reason there is the opposite concern on the side of organised criminals. It is possible to hypothesise that these collusive agreements are favoured in a combination with:

- systematic variables, such as a long competition with an inevitable spread of violence;

- organisational variables, such as weakness of the organisations due to infiltration, turncoats, convictions of the top leaders;

- economic variables, such as changes in the markets, reduction of resources, demand for specialisation;

- perception of an increase of law enforcement risks.

In this respect, two main questions need to be answered: first, are these collusive agreements among criminal groups increasing, that is, is the co-operation among criminal organisations developing? Second, is this cooperation tactical, that is, for carrying out a particular action or business, or strategic, that is, oriented towards a plurality of consequent actions, or is it a mixture of both?

There is a continuum from complete mergers between organisations at the one extreme to independent spot market transactions on an on-and-off basis at the other, so that these alliances can take many forms, including operating linkages, licensing or franchise agreements and joint ventures. Tactical arrangements, in this case, rather than strategic alliances are developed, because of the lack of long-term expectations. In many respects, such activities seem to be typical of a significant part of the drug-trafficking industry, that is, they are carried out by small, independent organisations that have come together to exploit a particular trafficking route and a specific way of circumventing customs and law enforcement. Not only are many of these small tactical alliances based on transnational networks, when they are effective they have an inherent capacity for growth. At the same time, their loose, fluid nature makes it equally plausible that they will be disbanded and their constituent elements re-formed in different constellations.

The development of alliances can be understood as a response by individual firms to the business environment, and as an attempt to overcome their own limitations. In the first place, alliances are the rational response to the creation of a common market and to the consequent multiplication of business opportunities. One of the most important ways to accomplish this is by aggressively gaining access to new markets.

The other way is to cooperate with those firms that are already entrenched in these markets, thus profiting from greater knowledge of local conditions, and being more attuned to local problems. In this case, alliances can also provide an effective means of circumventing restrictions posed by government or anti-governmental organisations which can make it difficult for foreign organisations to penetrate the market.

Closely related to this is another consideration, involving the desire to neutralise and even co-opt actual or potential competitors. Paradoxically, cooperative tactics offer a rational and effective response to a highly competitive situation. Obviously the organisations already in the market have to be offered something substantial in return, or some other form of reciprocity has to be exercised.

Cooperation among criminal organisations is often aimed at circumventing law enforcement and national regulations. From this perspective, it is clear that at least some of the alliances can be understood as risk-reduction alliances. Criminal organisations make alliances with governments, either through corruption or coercion or, more often, a mixture of both. A recurring feature of this behaviour is the extended use of bribery in Italy in order to enhance the control on the territory, to minimise the risk of law enforcement and to strengthen the organisations' position against external competitors. Another example is offered by the criminal networks carrying out EU or VAT frauds, which must necessarily develop ties with institutions both at a national and a European level.

4.6. (INCREASING) DEMAND AND OPPORTUNITIES FOR MONEY-LAUNDERING

The expansion of criminal activities considered is the starting point for assuming that the demand for money-laundering by criminal organisations will increase.

The European Union is a real unified financial market for clean operators, and a virtual one for criminals. If unification means more competition for legitimate industries, better quality and lower prices for European citizens, criminals perceive the trend toward unification in a contradictory way. On the one hand, they try to exploit the abolishment of borders, moving easily from one place to another On the other, they perceive the unification of the national markets as more risky because of higher cooperation and more control, and less protection in their own country. If we consider legitimate and criminal enterprises as faces of the same coin, we need to understand that what is an advantage for legitimate enterprises and for European citizens could be a risk for the criminal enterprises and for criminals.

In considering its effects in terms of an additional harmonisation of regulations and more effective controls upon the financial mechanisms, it is necessary to take into account the deviating role and the consequent special concern represented by neighbouring countries with special financial and economic relations with the EU (i.e. Liechtenstein, Switzerland, Eastern European countries). With different, or less stringent, financial regulations, they can offer to criminals a safe haven or entry point for further steps into the EU financial market. This creates a serious problem of identification for financial institutions located in countries with special links with these regions such as, for example, Finland, Sweden or Austria. Several of these countries have made money-laundering a punishable offence, and/or have taken steps to ensure that a banker is relieved of his duty of secrecy in order to permit a criminal investigation to proceed. However, they also have varying rules on disclosure of the true ownership of accounts, and of beneficial owners such as nominees or trustees or bearer shares.

Of special concern to European law enforcement agencies are also financial havens in the placement phase. A first category of these countries is in some ways linked to EU member countries because of specific historical, political or economic ties (the Channel Islands, the Isle of Man, Monaco). Some European banks recently set up local offices in these offshore centres. Worth mentioning in this respect are also the overseas former colonies of EU countries. They take advantage of special economic and financial relations with EU countries and, for this reason, can be considered as open doors for suspect capital which finds investment opportunities within the Union.

Other countries, such as Andorra, Gibraltar or Cyprus are preferred by money-launderers because of their close geographical proximity. Criminal groups or professionals acting as money-launderers open shell or front companies in such countries so that they can transmit money there through over-invoicing, in order to invest the capital in the European financial markets.

The existence of these secret havens has made currency smuggling, a traditional method, popular. Currency smuggling affords the launderer the advantage of completely expunging the trail between the criminal activity generating the funds and the actual placement of the proceeds in the financial system. These proceeds later return either to the country of origin or within the European financial investment markets by apparently legal methods.

Inside Europe, the methods of money-laundering are developing in relation to the controls exercised by financial authorities. The provision of stricter regulations and controls put in place by individual member countries as a consequence of the EU Directive on money-laundering, has also increased. This has caused the need for additional outlets to avoid the increased pressure from law enforcement agencies.

Still, in the majority of the European countries, legislation does not impose obligations on commercial enterprises. Commingling of illegally gained capital with deposits of an ostensibly legitimate commercial enterprise or corporate entity carries a low risk of detection. Criminals deal with a wide range of activities and use them in both the placement stage, as a destination for funds invested, and to create a legitimate layer for further commingling of illicit funds. At the layering and integration stages, launderers often operate making widespread use of front activities, with a continued preference for ultimately using banks in major financial centres as collection points or conduits for moving funds world-wide.

Front activities are set up by the Mafia in the South of Italy, and by local criminal networks in Belgium, with the purpose of using them within relatively short periods of time for criminal purposes such as money-laundering or financial fraud. They are subsequently liquidated or closed down, in order to conceal the documentation, and therefore the money trail.

Illicit proceeds are commingled with the legitimate funds of an enterprise and then represented as income from its legitimate activities. Unless a financial institution is suspicious of the transactions (for example, by re-alising that business receipts are too high as compared with the average rate of income of a particular sector), the commingling of illegal funds is difficult for law enforcement agencies to detect or for bank officials to suspect. Commingling is usually carried out through the method of false invoices or 'double invoicing'. It allows a legitimate justification for funds received from abroad. This method of laundering money has been widely reported by Italian law enforcement as a common practice of Italian criminals, and it is even emerging as a common trend among white-collar criminals in a number of other European countries. Shell or front compa-nies, often run by so-called men of straw, are set up by criminals, particu-larly in neighbouring offshore countries for that purpose only. The risk of discovery by law enforcement officers following investigations into the real nature of these entities cause these companies to disappear as quickly as they appeared.

A stricter legislation, putting financial institutions in a position which does not allow them to be easily used for laundering illicit proceeds, causes money-launderers to orient themselves more and more towards the use of financial institutions other than banks. There is evidence of crimi-nal groups moving away from the major commercial banks to those they think are less likely to report suspicious transactions; they often operate accounts in the name of offshore companies. These include a wide variety of 'bureaux de change', cheque-cashing services, insurers, brokers, im-porters, exporters and other trading companies, gold and precious metal dealers, courier services and other money movers of varying degrees of sophistication and capability. Casinos or gambling houses are also used at the placement stage. Enquiries into stock-markets have also revealed that much illicitly gained money is laundered in this circuit. A special mention has to be made of the fact that insurance companies are becoming in-creasingly popular laundering mechanisms. The use of more sophisticated money-laundering methods has gone also beyond wire transfers to include a seemingly endless variety of licit and illicit financial instruments.

The possibility for criminal organisations to launder their proceeds through banking financial institutions exists both without the knowledge by the financial or commercial operator of the illicit source, and with more or less explicit complicity. Individually or in concert, employees of finan-cial or business institutions are facilitating money-laundering operations by willingly accepting large cash deposits, by failing to report transactions which exceed the threshold required by the law, or by filing false reporting documents.

There is emerging concern about new banking practices within the European Union, such as direct access banking (favoured customers are given the bank's software and allowed to process transactions directly through their accounts) or suspense accounts (of banks with other banks). Pass-through banking by itself is posing a myriad of problems for regulators, by creating accounts within accounts, even banks within banks. These new banking services limit the utility of identification systems. Representative offices (a Rep office is an office representing a foreign bank that does not have a branch in a specific country) constitute another favoured medium used by money-launderers. Normal financial regulations do not always apply to them because such an office is not considered to be an official banking institute, while the office accepts deposits and transfers the funds into its own account without disclosing the identities of the beneficial owners of the deposits.

Furthermore a new category of professional money-laundering specialists is emerging. They sell high quality services, contacts, experience and knowledge of money movements, supported by the latest electronic technology, especially in international financial centres such as Germany or the United Kingdom, to any trafficker or other criminal willing to pay their fees.

In addition to buying into established companies, or creating shell corporations in out-of-the-way places, and buying and trading commodities, purchasing equipment, and the like, the more sophisticated money managers put the traffickers' proceeds into a wide range of financial instruments. The possibilities offered by important international financial and stock exchange centres in the EU comprise an endless variety of possibilities for diversification. They often manage funds for third parties beyond contracts such as fiduciary contracts, financial management, foundations, third party accounts and new typologies of contracts such as trust companies. Professionals number criminal organisations among their many clients, and make available to them the same mechanisms used by other clients to smuggle gold or to hide profits and shelter proceeds from the tax collector. In a variation on this procedure, some money brokers are buying cash in bulk, at a discount rate. The criminal organisations get their proceeds back from the point-of-sale countries without having the burden of making the moves themselves.

11. ORGANISATIONAL CRIME; THE SITUATION IN GERMANY

H. Maass

1. Introduction

Organised crime control is a key aspect of the issue of internal security in Europe. Organised criminals take advantage of the rights of law-abiding citizens in order to engage in illegal activities without interference. The public is right in expecting the criminal justice authorities to take vigorous counter-measures. At the same time, the public also plays an important role when it comes to organised crime control. For that reason they must be part of any measure geared to combating this form of crime.

In establishing special organised crime offices throughout the country in most recent years, comprehensive organisational structures have been created to meet the ever-increasing demands in the battle against organised crime.

Annual *Situation Reports on Organised Crime* (OC) have been compiled in Germany since 1991. They have proven worthwhile in the quantitative and qualitative assessment of the phenomenon. Only on the basis of reliable information reflecting the extent and the manifestations of organised crime:

- can focal points be identified;

- is a targeted-oriented use of resources and manpower possible;

- can necessary changes of law in the field of criminal policy be initiated, and

- can the public be supplied with appropriate situation data in order to build a broad consensus of opinion in favour of law enforcement's needs in all strata of society.

The *Situation Report on Organised Crime* is a survey of all OC-related cases handled by the police, that concentrates on fundamental aspects of the information gathered and that is based on a common definition of organised crime and an information-gathering system developed specifically for this purpose.

2. The 1995 Condensed Situation Report on Organised Crime

2.1. ORGANISED CRIME: A HIGHLY COMPLEX PHENOMENON

Regarding problems of information-gathering and validity of conclusions, the following points should be kept in mind when judging the information presented in the 1995 Situation Report:

- Organised crime cannot be described in terms of clearly definable legal elements that constitute individual offences, but is rather a highly complex phenomenon. The results presented here are based primarily on information obtained from investigations, which means the present report deals with organised crime activity that has already been detected. It is not possible to make statements about unreported activity in the field of organised crime on the basis of the data collected.

- Organised crime does not operate in the open. Therefore organised crime can often only be identified on the basis of active information-gathering and professional analysis of the data obtained. The legal situation and/or inadequate staffing often limit what can be accomplished in this connection.

- The accuracy of any forecast about probable developments in the field of organised crime on the basis of the data collected therefore is limited.

2.2. QUANTITATIVE DATA

Nearly 800 investigations of organised crime were conducted in the Federal Republic of Germany in 1995. The investigations analysed contained information on about 8,000 suspects who committed a total of 52,000 individual offences in 1995. More than 40,000 OC suspects have been investigated since 1991. During this period they caused known material losses amounting to almost 10.5 billion DM. This is one example of the threat posed by organised crime. In the other areas of crime where no direct material damage results (or cannot be measured), profits since 1991 are estimated at over 4.1 billion DM. In addition, various types of organised crime (e.g. drug-related and environmental crime, crime involving weapons, trafficking in human beings) cause an enormous amount of material and non-material damage each year that cannot be quantified. Besides this, the large profits obtained by illegal means serve as 'investment capital' for further criminal activity, and help criminal organisations continue to grow in power and influence.

2.3. QUALITATIVE DATA
The international dimension

With regard to more than two thirds of the investigations, offences were committed in other countries as well as in Germany. The results of the respective analyses confirm that the OC groups identified are active all over the world. Evidently national borders do not represent an insurmountable obstacle for them. The international criminal activity is concentrated in Europe, in particular in the countries that have common borders with Germany, and in countries associated with certain crimes and ways of committing them – for example, drug-trafficking and smuggling in Turkey. Organised crime groups continue to use Europe as a unified economic and operational area.

In many cases there are also connections between OC groups active in Germany and established criminal organisations in foreign countries, for example the Sicilian Mafia, the Colombian drug cartels, the 'Russian Mafia', or the Kurdish PKK.

The fact that the percentage of non-German suspects has risen steadily, from 50.6% in 1991 to 63.6% in 1995 serves to underline the international nature of organised crime. The percentage of suspects who came from Eastern Europe increased from 10.6% in 1993 to 12.8% in 1994 and to 14% in 1995.

The exploitation of commercial structures

One significant threat posed by organised crime is its systematic exploitation of the flexibility of economic and legal systems and the many possibilities for manipulating them. Legal business structures provide an ideal basis for illegal transactions. At the same time, the fact that it is often difficult to trace the path taken by financial transactions makes it possible to cover up crimes committed in this connection. In 1995, commercial structures were exploited in Germany with regard to half the investigations analysed, and in foreign countries with regard to almost a quarter of the investigations. Business-like structures were exploited in almost a quarter of the investigations in Germany and in almost a seventh of the respective investigations in foreign countries.

The use of violence

Intimidation and force continue to play a major role with regard to achievement of criminal objectives and securing claims to power, even though increasingly subtle methods can be observed as the degree of organisation increases. Use of force was identified in almost a quarter of the investigations analysed in Germany. Other means of intimidation were employed in Germany with regard to almost one third of the investigations. Compared to 1994, the share of OC investigations in Germany associated with the use of force was reduced by half. In a similar manner, the number of recorded violent crimes has declined for the first time since 1991. However, it is doubtful that this can be viewed as indicating that OC groups are now less prone to violence. The forms of intimidation and use of force range from direct and indirect threats to torture and murder. They include bodily assault and injury as well as warning shots, robberies, arson, detonation of hand grenades, threatening, mistreating and abducting family members, and carrying out fake executions. Such intimidation not only has an impact on the specific criminal or civil proceedings but also has the intended effect on other proceedings as well. When statements by the persons involved are lacking, it is often not possible to produce evidence in OC investigations.

In more than one-eighth of OC investigations, it was necessary to place endangered persons in the witness protection programme.

Bribery, corruption and extortion

The instruments used by OC perpetrators to safeguard their position of power include subtle forms of exerting influence in the areas of politics, public administration, and justice, as well as the business sector. Among other things, influence is exerted by means of bribery, extortion or coercion. Those working in public administration are the most common targets of influence exerted by OC perpetrators. In Germany, influence on public administration could be demonstrated in one tenth of the investigations. With regard to 33 of the 1995 OC investigations, acts of corruption came to light. The information that the police have on acts of corruption, especially those linked to organised crime, must still be regarded as fairly limited. However, the *Situation Report on Corruption* in the Federal Republic of Germany in 1994 does provide, for the first time, representative information on what is known about crime in this area. Regardless of the kind of influence exerted – be it threats, the use of force, or corruption – it is above all the public's faith in government institutions, as well as in a functioning state governed by the rule of law and, last but not least, its sense of security that are severely shaken by such forms of crime.

2.4. SPECIALISATION IN LAW ENFORCEMENT

There was further professionalisation of activity in the battle against organised crime during the reported period. The percentage of investigations handled by special organised crime offices increased from about 51% in 1994 to about 57% in 1995. At the same time, the percentage of proceedings pending with the public prosecutor's offices specialising in organised crime increased from about 46% in 1994 to about 52% in 1995.

Furthermore, the fact that money-laundering activity is being detected to an increasing extent in connection with investigative proceedings demonstrates the increasingly significant role played by financial investigations as an integral part of such proceedings. Perpetrators associated with organised crime are involved in almost all areas of criminal activity.

2.5. SOME RESULTS

The largest group of non-German suspects comprises Turkish nationals (1,153 or 14.6%). Vietnamese nationals accounted for an above-average share of the armed suspects (19.4%). Losses of about 673 million DM were established in 1995, along with additional estimated profits of approximately 718 million DM. More than two-thirds of the investigations analysed were characterised by criminal offences committed at international level. In approximately one-fourth of investigations, links to the Netherlands were discovered, while in almost one-sixth of such investigations there were links to Poland.

3. Organised Crime committed by criminal groups from the former Soviet Union

3.1. THE 'RUSSIAN MAFIA'

Only part of the organised crime groups often referred to as the 'Russian Mafia' in the media originate in Russia. Most of them come from the Ukraine, Georgia, Azerbaijan, Armenia, Lithuania, Latvia and the Chechenian Republic. Some of these groups have existed for a longer period of time, while others were formed after the collapse of the Communist system.

3.2. ACTIVITIES IN GERMANY

Criminal organisations from the territory of the former Soviet Union were also engaged in illegal acts in Germany. A distinction must be made between groups operating at regional level and groups originally based in the former Soviet Union which have meanwhile established international links. The majority of persons at the command level of known organisations from the former Soviet Union were born there, but became citizens of either a Western European or North American country some time ago. So far, criminal groups from Russia, Chechenia, Lithuania, Georgia, the Ukraine, Armenia and Azerbaijan have been identified in Germany. Looking at the whole of Germany, they were primarily engaged in trafficking in human beings, extortion, trafficking in stolen vehicles and money-laundering. Until their withdrawal in August 1994, members of the so-called Western Group of Russian Forces in Germany participated in various criminal activities in Germany such as fraud, tax evasion, trafficking in stolen vehicles and crime involving weapons. Examples from Dresden and Halle serve to prove that in the new Federal states of Germany, criminal groups from the former Soviet Union are above all made up of ex-members of the Western Group of Russian Forces stationed in Germany. In many cases, the set-up of these groups reflects ethnic origin. They have a hierarchical structure, and the members collaborate, each with appointed tasks. In addition, import/export companies are increasingly being established by members of these groups, with their objectives being any type of trade. At this time it is not possible to say if there has been an influx of illegally obtained funds into these companies.

The offender structure is different in the old Federal states of former West Germany. Here we find violent offenders, but also criminals exploiting commercial structures for illegal purposes. More and more often police have to deal with Russians in exile who rely on established business structures, as well as with businessmen from the former Soviet Union who are believed to be in contact with criminal organisations or to carry out instructions given by them. Berlin is regarded as the centre of organised crime of (what used to be) Soviet origin. In most Federal states, criminal groups have surfaced who have known contacts to Berlin. In some cases links were established to criminal organisations identified by the Russian authorities and operating at international level.

4. Financial investigations

For some time now, the fight against money-laundering as part of organised crime has been a central issue in the controversial debate about internal security by politics and society. The majority of persons and groups involved do not operate in the open, and often illegal activities are mingled with legal business activities. It is this combination of legal and illegal activities that makes it difficult for the criminal justice authorities to describe the overall phenomenon of money-laundering and, eventually, to win the battle against it. In late November 1993 the Money-laundering Act came into force. It is meant to implement the EC Directives of 10.06.91 and, in certain cases, requires banks and other institutions to identify customers and to report suspicious transactions to the criminal justice authorities.

When it comes to assessing this legislation, the following aspects must be taken into account: When dealing with organised crime – and money-laundering is a critical part of organised crime – the usual assessment criteria such as clear-up rates are either not suitable or practicable. Short-term success is not possible. This is due to the highly complex nature of cases, but also to the enormous demands made on the criminal justice authorities when collecting evidence in this field of crime.

The German Code of Criminal Procedure causes further problems for the police. For example, the issue of surveillance of telecommunications in cases of suspected money-laundering activity (money-laundering is not part of the catalogue of offences listed in Section 100a of the German Code of Criminal Procedure) or the restrictive interpretation in connection with undercover investigations. In addition, it is in fact difficult to trace and to comprehend complex financial transactions, which must always be seen in an international context and are sometimes carried out by highly specialised members of criminal organisations.

To handle these manifold problems, joint financial investigation teams of police and customs were set up in Germany at a national and Federal state level. A task force has also been established at the Bundeskriminalamt (BKA) in Wiesbaden. It consists of officers from the BKA and the Customs Investigations Office (ZKA). In 1994, a total of 3,282 reports of suspicious transactions was filed with the appropriate criminal justice authorities, and in particular the Criminal Police Offices of the Federal states. The volume of suspicious transactions carried out was in the region of 1.4 million DM. It is, however, noteworthy that most of this money part cannot be clearly identified as being legal or illegal money.

Suspicious transaction reports by financial institutions were mainly based on the following criteria:

- type and volume of the transaction;

- the identity of the customer;

- the country where the beneficiary's account was located;

- The quality of suspicious transaction reports increased in as much as the institutions involved followed the so-called know-your-customer principle.

In 1994 a total of 2,738 investigative proceedings were initiated for a suspected violation of Section 261 of the German Penal Code. 1,014 of these proceedings were discontinued (37%). The allegation of money-laundering could only be substantiated in about 4% of the remaining proceedings. In most of these cases the money originated from drug-related crime.

The results of the *Situation Reports on Financial Investigations* for 1994 and 1995 are fully comparable in most cases. There was a 10.5% decline in the number of initial reports about suspected money-laundering activity (2,935), but several Federal states found that there was a considerable increase in quality of suspicious transactions reports received there. In 1995 about 10,395,000 DM worth of assets were confiscated as a result of investigations opened on the grounds of suspicious transactions reports. Also in 1995, about 1,880,000 DM-worth of assets confiscated was released. German suspects were at the top of the list, followed by Turkish and Russian nationals.

Anti-money-laundering legislation and appropriate police concepts should not be judged in terms of failure or success, but as a first step towards winning the battle against internationally organised crime. However, this first step must be followed by further innovative steps which go beyond traditional methods of law enforcement.

12. THE SERIOUS CRIME THREATS IN THE UNITED KINGDOM

D.C. Veness

1. Introduction

Organised and serious crime within the United Kingdom (UK) will be dealt with here in terms of terrorism. As an example of contemporary terrorism the bomb-explosion on the 9th of February 1996 at South Key in the Docklands in London should be mentioned. Two people were killed here and forty-nine people were injured. The bomb used was a so-called 'Large Vehicle Improvised Explosive Device' (LVIED), containing a massive quantity of home-made explosives detonated less than an hour and a half after the end of the cease-fire by the Provisional Irish Republican Army and after a precise warning was delivered. The scale of the explosion can be illustrated by the fact that it was possible to walk for fifteen minutes in any direction and not to leave an area in which one might have been killed. It impressed upon Scotland Yard the need to re-educate our officers concerning the need for four-hundred meter cordons around such a Large Vehicle Improvised Explosive Device.

The main responsibility of a senior police officer engaged in encountering terrorism, apart from personal leadership, is to ensure effective cooperation and coordination between agencies. Counter-terrorism is inevitably multi-dimensional, therefore cooperation between agencies is absolutely critical.

Public disputes are corrosive and serve only the interest of the terrorists. The media are like circling vultures in this area, and publish very few reports of good cooperation. Still, there is an excellent relationship between British police and our Security and Intelligence Services. Excellent international links have also been established. Most striking at the moment is the link between London and Paris, both being engaged in disrupting the logistic support of the armed Islamic group GIA, an Algerian focused organisation which carried out murderous attacks in France last summer.

These attacks were aimed at crowded public places (underground railway stations), and all occurred without warning of any kind.

2. Forms of domestic terrorism

People in the UK are resigned to the long-term threat of the murderous activities of the provisional IRA. Their cease-fires should be seen as periods of terrorist preparation, and the last period of preparation ended on the 9th of February. After that, six attacks have been executed in London, the last just one month ago aimed at a major bridge near central London. Other Irish threats emanate from the Irish National Liberation Army (INLA), and on the other side of the sectarian divide from those who operate under the name of 'Loyalists'. On the international front London, and to an extent the whole of the UK, is an international crossroads of terrorist and protest activity. Primary concerns are also with Middle-Eastern rejectionist groups, those who would reject peace and seek to eliminate the state of Israel. Bombs were delivered against the Israeli Embassy and against an Israeli community centre on the 26th and 27th of July 1994, and persons await trial for those offences. Terrorist threats also come from South-Asia, from the PKK engaged in extortion activities, and special interest arises from the phenomenon of the Afghan groups, those who are bonded in conflicts which seem to cross divisions within Islam. Activities emanating from Bosnia also deserve special attention. To complete the international picture, state-sponsored threats arise primarily from Iran, and increasingly from Libya. Iran is particularly poignant in the context of the UK because of its responsibility to protect the author Salman Rushdie.

A last single issue, a batch of issues actually, regards such forms as animal extremism, environmental extremism and new religious movements. Next to this is the question as to what particularly the activities regarding the Chemical and Biological production and even millenarianism will mean in terms of the development from terrorism to that of organised crime.

Nevertheless, the threat to the UK is overwhelmingly the large amount of local crime that continues to be the dominant picture within the forensic map of this country. These are the crimes which are easy to recognise: burglary, crime addressed against vehicles, and street violence, unhappily with increasing firearms incidents, unusual in an unarmed society as the UK is known to be.

3. Overseas influences

All of the enterprises are to a certain degree represented in the UK. Certainly Mafia, and increasing links to Central and Eastern Europe can be found. Elsewhere, beyond Europe, the Colombian cartels, Nigerian influences, both in terms of drugs and a massive input to fraud, and West Indian activity are not unfamiliar. Regarding the latter, the UK is part of a triangle that links the Caribbean, the eastern coastal borders of the United States and the major cities here. And lastly there are local and overseas links. Examples include fraud linking London and Moscow, drugs going to Southern Europe, and indeed English lorry drivers are highly valued for their determination in the Balkans. They always get the loads through, which is perhaps our least meritorious export to Europe.

4. A multi-disciplinary, multi-agency and multinational approach

The operational philosophy sought to operate against these threats is based on what has been described by the FBI as follows: "No single law enforcement agency anywhere acting alone has ever sustained an attack on organised crime". Individual cases: yes; some successful task forces: yes. But not a sustained campaign. Operating on a multi-disciplinary, a multi-agency and a multinational basis is required. On a multinational basis it is recognised that policing within the UK is part of European law enforcement. The same problems are shared in this respect. Overwhelmingly, the examples are trade in drugs, but also vehicles on the move (not only private vehicles, but commercial vehicles as well), plants, arts, antiques, computer parts, and indeed people themselves in terms of a range of offences including illegal immigration.

5. Responses to an increasing mobility in crime

Mobility of people and property in Europe inevitably provides increasing criminal opportunities. The speed of criminal enterprises, the speed with which crime has taken advantage of mobility exceeds the reaction of the law enforcement response. Certainly amongst police officers, but among legal structures as well, there is need for fast-track action and cooperation between divergent legal traditions. It is also the case that some serious crimes follow population movements, not only literally, in terms of persons on the move, but also movement in a political and social sense. An agenda is required to counter this particular threat. First and foremost, it should be recognised that there is a problem and that this problem is a shared one. Therefore a multi-agency path, in which everyone expects and accepts responsibility, is required. Building our political defences is an issue here. Countries which, for example, are devoid of a democratic tradition and integrity will inevitably be hotbeds of international crime. Contemporary examples of this situation can certainly be found in West Africa. There is a need for professional ethics in the world of banking, accountancy and business, as well as a need to identify and defend the predictable weak areas: gambling, prostitution, illegal immigration, and extortion. And, last but not least, there is a need for effective law enforcement. Law enforcement is critical to the debate and a bottom-up, top-down approach should be considered. The argument is that law enforcement activities inevitably need to be based upon local enforcement. Effective local enforcement is the bedrock for all further activities, of which national criminal intelligence facilities are one. A broadly based, multi-agency approach and innovative techniques are other important aspects. The latter is to be understood in terms of lawful audacity with the use of undercover and technical activities.

Within the UK, history is based upon local tradition and ad hoc solutions have been followed over the years, dating back to the previous century, to address serious crime. In recent years could be witnessed the evolution of larger regional crime squads and a national criminal intelligence service. We are on the threshold of achieving a national crime squad that will operate in partnership with a national criminal intelligence service (ENSIS). This will be our bridge to the world, linking our important connections with Europol, of which we are a member, and Interpol, of which we have been a member for many years. And increasingly we will be benefiting from the surveillance, technical and analytical capability of our own security service; legislation is being passed to bring that into effect. Turning to specific action, especially technical facilities, an increasing challenge follows from the fact that commerce and the pursuit of profit, particularly in terms of mobile telephony, has run ahead of the legislative provisions for law enforcement to make an impact. A gap, also spotted by the Director of the FBI, Louis Freed, that also exists in Europe. As to surveillance, human and technical, easy movement of surveillance activity has to be achieved, particularly where undercover operations across European borders are involved, even amongst the European borders of the 15 states of the European Union. In order to make any progress on confiscation of illegal capital, every serious crime investigation should have a parallel financial investigation. Another important aspect concerns witness protection, or indeed criminal justice protection, since not only witnesses, but also judges and juries are put at risk. Evidential use of informants as in the Italian model of the penitent offenders, informant-systems, and analytical techniques are probably the easiest of the law enforcement facilities to cross national borders. Tribute should also be paid to Europol for its path-finding work in providing cross-border analytical techniques that will serve law enforcement well. We also need to think in terms of fighting behind the lines. This is not quite the Churchillian notion of setting Europe ablaze, but is seeking to benefit from the inevitable fear that exists in the mind of the criminal. Let us stoke that fear and generate constructive paranoia through a fear of surveillance, be it human or intelligence. Activities should also be devoted to frustrating the logistic roots of criminal movements, we can disrupt, we can prevent, we can attack profits and we can also detect and prosecute.

The realisation exists in the UK that one way to achieve things is to form a joint action group (JAG) on a voluntary basis. The JAG brings together 27 separate agencies and groups, not all in the government service, not all from the official world. It is hoped that the endeavours for which the JAG has laid the foundation will be a useful supplement to the work of the national crime squad. The JAG meets roughly every three months, and defines strategic issues of importance, for example how to work with Central and Eastern European colleagues, and what is the nature of the threat within the United Kingdom. It identifies specific targets, enterprise groups of criminals; it seeks to identify task-forces, normally drawn from the regional crime squad, but also from the ranks of Customs and Excise and any other agencies that will lead and take forward investigations. Prevention strategies are designed, and some of these have achieved considerable success. Other examples of current cases that are dealt with by the JAG are West African fraud, primarily emanating from Nigeria, vehicle crime, and the prevention and detection of criminal activities around computer parts.

6. Kidnappings: a special case

Finally, a specific category of crime that is of particular concern, namely kidnappings and extortion, will be dealt with here. This kind of crime has to be considered as a growing challenge to law enforcement, because traditional and well-developed mechanisms which have served us so well for some time, are now under strain due to criminal sophistication. Such sophistication is based on mobility. Kidnap crimes, which existed in one particular locality, are now seen to be moving to areas where these had not been a significant problem before. We see cross-border issues where kidnappers seize a victim in one location and make their demands across the border. Kidnappers also try to make use of non-complementary national procedures by moving ransom payments across borders, often by means of electronic fund transfers. So kidnapping and extortion are crimes which cry out for an international and indeed a multi-disciplinary response. In this respect, mention should be made of a conference held in Moscow, involving three agencies: the Ministry of the Interior from Russia, the FBI and Scotland Yard. Here some of the particular problems in this field were identified, and lessons were learned from Russian colleagues, whose case history under this heading at the moment is regrettably considerable. It should be emphasised that there is more scope for European cooperation in relation to the specifics of kidnappings and extortion.

7. Conclusion

All sorts of European law enforcement structures should be built. These must be nationally based, however, and must be founded on national political and legal structures. On these foundations the benefits of international cooperation could be constructed. The classic example is Europol, which can be defined as a house with sixteen rooms. One room is located in The Hague, its headquarters, but the important rooms are the fifteen others within the national capitals of the European Union (EU), and they classically are within the national criminal intelligence centres of the fifteen capitals of the EU. Those who perform best, and the French and Germans lead the way in this respect, achieve this by co-locating the Europol office with an Interpol office, thus achieving effective international convergence with Europol. For law enforcement to be successful in dealing with organised crime it should even go beyond European borders to the wider international context. I would suggest that we, as chiefs of law enforcement, need to build upon the foundations of successful national endeavours to reach a geographic vision that transcends the borders of our own force, to see beyond the borders of our own region and indeed beyond our countries, and recognise the need for organisational convergence which will be essential for regional and global activity. International cooperation hitherto has been built upon bilateral arrangements that served us well in the post-war era, but the political, social and legal structures are growing ever more sophisticated. May I suggest that our responsibility as the leaders of law enforcement in Europe and elsewhere is to think about how we will enter the multilateral era. The title of this conference being policing the future, I would suggest that our agenda is moving to multilateral structures and multilateral cooperation.

13. THE FBI'S PERSPECTIVE OF ORGANISED CRIME

A.G. Ringgold

1. Defining organised crime

The FBI's operating definition of organised crime is '*a continuing criminal conspiracy, having an organised structure, fed by fear and corruption and motivated by greed*'. That is an expansive definition, reflecting the realities experienced in the United States. It is a definition which allows for sufficient fluidity to include the many new emerging groups which we are experiencing in our society.

We Americans take pride in the 'melting pot' nature of our country. An unfortunate by-product of that feature though is that virtually every known organised criminal group operating in the world has its representatives in the USA. Our organised criminal problem reflects our cultural diversity. It reflects the freedoms available to the residents of the country. It reflects the incredible rate of shrinkage of the world, with instantaneous communications, ready access to international travel, globalisation of economies, and criss-crossing waves of immigration. The changes in Central and Eastern Europe and in the People's Republic of China have energised long controlled and relatively benign criminal groups, which today are coming on line as major participants in the global spread of criminality.

The purpose here is to provide insight concerning the American experience with organised crime, and our perspective of what can be successful in combating it. Still, it is to be recognised that these experiences may be vastly different from each of the other countries'. In this respect two thoughts must be kept in mind when taking note of the FBI's perspective:

- if the fact is accepted that organised criminal activity is globalising, the absolute necessity to work with other countries in combating it will be understood. The concept of developing law enforcement partnerships, working jointly and fluidly against mutual problems, is wholeheartedly subscribed to by the FBI.

- Unfortunately it is normally a reality that trends often start in the United States. The USA has an uncanny knack of exporting its life-style – good and bad – and its problems. Many of the problems the USA faces will shortly become problems in other countries as well.

2. Criminal groups active in the United States

What follows is a description of the criminal groups which exist in the United States and how they are dealt with.

Italian groups

La Cosa Nostra
The Camorra
The 'Ndrangheta
The Sacred Crown

There are several thousand hard-core criminals in the United States who represent all of these groups. Each member of these groups is a career-dedicated criminal, whose sole activities are criminal. They act individually, in concert with other members of their own organisation, and across the lines of the organised groups. Their illegal activity runs the entire gamut of crime. It includes drug-trafficking, murders, bribery, gambling, prostitution, frauds, extortion, and rampant corruptive influence in many sectors of our society. Among the most flagrant and destructive of their illegal activities is the illegal domination of several of our national labour unions. It is taken as axiomatic that they exert tremendous illegal influence on the Teamsters, the labourers international, the hotel and restaurant workers, and on the longshoremen. In fact, although it cannot specifically be quantified, it can be concluded that a significant portion of what Americans pay for most commodities in the United States is added by virtue of the criminal activities.

The FBI's attention to the Italian groups was delayed. For many years the official position was one of denial that the groups existed pervasively in the United States. In 1956 an event occurred in Appalachian, New York, which finally captured the attention and jogged the FBI into action. On that occasion, a New York state police officer encountered a 'Mafia summit' in a small town in that state. That disclosure of a national network of criminals spurred the FBI into action. At that time it was frustrating to realise that there were no legislative tools to utilise in a combat against the

Italian criminals. The FBI worked laboriously with the US Congress to have the appropriate laws enacted. Finally, in 1970, the Bureau was sufficiently outfitted with laws and manpower to make a dedicated commitment to the fight. New authorities to wire-tap and seize property could be used from then on. Also a legislative jewel, referred to as the RICO statute (Racketeer Influenced and Corrupt Organisations Statute), was created. Gradually the FBI's entire philosophy of fighting organised criminal activity changed. From an agency that addressed single instances of criminality, it became one that recognised that there was strength to be found in addressing criminal enterprises or conspiracies. In that vein, efforts were entirely retooled. Over the ensuing years, notable successes against the Italians could be registered. Many hundreds of the managers of the groups were imprisoned, and their activities disrupted. Seizure statutes were utilised, and in some instances civil suits were filed against labour unions, forcing them to take on government-appointed managers to rid them of criminal penetration. Thus groups were literally devastated. Still, we are not under any illusion that they are defeated. Quite the contrary. Paradoxically, we have in some way contributed to the complexity of the problem today. The traditional La Cosa Nostra families in the United States were very structured. They had a boss, a *consigliere*, an underboss, capos and soldiers. Everyone had a specific mission and specific orders to fulfil it. If anyone got out of line, there were varying degrees of sanction available. Certain mores were ingrained. No-one dealt in drugs. No-one messed with the ladies of fellow members. No-one protested orders given to them by superiors. No-one took vengeance on police officials...especially not the FBI. Now the situation has changed, and in some ways reflects the changes in society in general. The groups are fragmented, with no definable chain of command. Discipline no longer exists in the ranks. Orders are often challenged by the rank and file members of the groups. Rather than calmly and coolly committing criminal acts, the groups are much more prone to spontaneous violence. Drug-trafficking is a staple of their revenue. And very troubling for the FBI is the fact that the traditional sacrosanct police officer and FBI agent is now considered relatively fair game.

The FBI, together with the Italian police services, also attacked Italian organised crime. But it was not until 1981 that structured dialogue with the Italian services commenced; these were designed to identify and address commonalties in criminal problems as they were experienced in both countries. From that date, this relationship improved through individual investigations, gradually building trust on both sides. Today, a point has been reached with the three Italian services and with their judiciary where one can speak of true partnership, doing joint wire-taps, undercover investigations, protecting each other's witnesses, and testifying in each other's courts. Dr. Giovanni Falcone was the symbol of this great relationship. When he was killed in Sicily, FBI agents participated fully in the investigation of the bombing. In fact, the FBI is quite proud that a major part of the evidence that is currently being presented in the Italian courts is FBI-developed evidence. The bust of Dr. Falcone stands in a small courtyard at the FBI-Academy in Quantico, Virginia, reminding everyone of his superstar status and of the super relationship between the law enforcement agencies of both countries.

Asian criminal groups

The Asian groups have their origins in most of the countries of the Orient. This includes Chinese (both the People's Republic and Taiwan), Vietnamese, Japanese and Korean. Legal and illegal immigration from the oriental countries is very high. It is encouraged by the USA. Most of the immigrants contribute heavily to the economy and the cultural diversity. Among the many immigrants are criminal entrepreneurs. Thinking of the Orient as being extremely intelligent and efficient in normal life, it can be understand that the challenge Asians pose when they engage in criminal activities is a severe one. They are involved in the entire gamut of criminal activity, but generally are much more violent than the Italians. An exacerbating factor is also their ethnocentricity. They generally spend the first one or two generations in cultural ghettos. They are linguistically isolated, which, for criminals, is an asset. The victims of their criminality are often their ethnic community. Their very efficient system of money-laundering through family members, without the actual transfer of funds, makes their crimes virtually impossible to detect. They are difficult to infiltrate because of their traditional reliance on blood relationships. There is also a preponderant reluctance to wander outside their cultural cocoon, to report crimes committed upon them by their ethnic brothers, or to provide information to non-oriental police services about acts which occur inside their enclaves. One of the techniques utilised judiciously but commonly by the FBI is undercover investigation. Here, very limited success in thoroughly infiltrating these groups can be reported. On the contrary, meaningful relationships could be forged with most of the law enforcement services in the Orient, resulting in never-ending cooperative ventures. Imagine having the People's Republic of China prosecute a Chinese citizen for criminal acts committed in the United States. That occurred recently. The results of our investigation in the United States were formally provided to the Chinese procuratorate, and a Chinese process ensued. It has also become very common for China to assist the FBI by arresting and deporting Asian-American criminals who are being sought for crimes committed in the USA. The Orient presents other challenges. Laws of the countries of the region regularly diverge from those of the western world. For instance, organised crime in Japan has a different societal connotation than in the USA. The police are constrained from providing truly substantive information to foreign agencies concerning Japanese citizens in joint investigations. Slowly the FBI is succeeding in finding manners of overcoming these hurdles.

Citizens of the Orient are the second most prolific group of immigrants in the United States. It is becoming increasingly crucial to better understand them, and to forge better police-to-police relationships with their countries of origin.

Nigerian criminal groups

Who hasn't seen a letter from a Nigerian proposing a joint venture or an investment opportunity? As in Europe, the United States is flooded with Nigerian criminals. This phenomenon has occurred within the past several years, and has forced us to focus more and more resources on the problem. It is way beyond the archetypal Nigerian letter of solicitation for investments. They are now proficient drug-traffickers, international con artists, with imaginative schemes in insurance frauds, credit card frauds, and student-loan frauds. Financial institutions loose millions to their schemes, though this seems relatively obvious considering the never-ending stream of innovative techniques to commit fraud. Several years back, agents from the Drug Enforcement Administration worked with the Swiss authorities to devise an effective profile for use at Zurich Airport to predict the carriers of drugs from Nigeria. The profile proved so effective that the Swiss jails were soon full of Nigerians who had been caught in transit from Nigeria to New York carrying heroin in various forms. That reality prompted a comment by a Swiss police officer that it made little economic sense for the Swiss to perform the arrests in Switzerland. It would have been better for them to simply allow the Americans to follow their own profile in New York. It certainly would have saved the Swiss a lot of money.

Eurasian criminal groups

Perhaps the most difficult and protracted crime problem the United States faces today is coming from the countries of the former Soviet Union. Not one of the countries of North America or Western Europe is spared these emerging groups. Perhaps the United States' experience is the most egregious. It is the FBI's perception that these groups see the US as a country of great opportunity (or perhaps vulnerability), and as the age-old enemy who might still be brought to its knees by another form of attack. The FBI initiated its major focus on Eurasian organised crime in 1992. Eurasian criminal gangs have been active in the US since the early 1970s, but it was not until the breakup of the Soviet Union that the groups began to proliferate in Europe, and to expand into the West. It began in the US with the influx of Jewish *émigrés* from Russia. Among the 200,000 or so immigrants, we estimate that there were about 2,000 criminals. These have formed the nucleus of what today is a major problem. At least 25 formal Eurasian gangs operating in our country have been identified, and the number continues to increase. In 1994, the then First Deputy Minister of the Interior of Russia, General Mikhail Yegorov, was asked to testify before the Congress with Director Freeh. He testified that in 1990 his services had identified about 785 criminal groups in Russia. By 1994 that number had reached 8,059, with about 35,000 members. That is exponential growth! The Russians have an interesting term to characterise their major organised criminals: 'thieves in law.' They estimate that these number approximately 800. They are the elite of criminals, wielding extreme power and influence throughout regions of their countries. These 'thieves-in-law' act as something of a board of directors, loosely arbitrating disputes among criminal groups and providing guidance when key criminals are arrested. Another apparent reality of the Eurasian gangs is their shadowy relationship with members of the law enforcement and secret services of the Soviet Union. There are numerous indicators that officers who had worked clandestinely for the Soviet government have now retooled and are now key elements of the criminal groups. The trade craft which they so effectively used against the West is now being once again applied toward the same end.

Since 1992, the FBI's approach to the Eurasian gangs has changed. Initially we had to rely entirely on traditional police techniques. We struggled with the development of informants and witnesses in our territory, frankly with very moderate success. It became obvious almost immediately that, in order to understand the criminal activity on our own territory, we needed to devise a method by which we could quantify its origins in the former Soviet states. It was obvious that the only way to do that was to forge partnerships with the police services of those countries. In this respect, a fascinating conversation with a Finnish colleague can be referred to. He clearly articulated his frustration in dealing with the Russian police in St Petersburg. His attempts to develop a dialogue with his Russian colleagues were met with a new face each time he travelled to Russia for the meetings. Though the FBI had similar experiences, efforts are beginning to pay off now. A major cooperative effort has been undertaken with the Russians, the law enforcement agencies of the three Baltic states, with the Ukraine, the Slovak and Czech republics, the Polish, the Hungarians, the Romanians, the Kazakhs, the Uzbeks, and soon with the remaining countries. In February, Director Freeh travelled to the Davos, Switzerland Economic Forum, where he had meetings with numerous heads of state from Central and Eastern Europe. Their universal theme was a need to deal with their rapidly advancing criminality, and the fact that they did not have the wherewithal to accomplish this alone. Each and every one of them urged the director to forge a meaningful relationship with their police services, and pledged full cooperation in a global law enforcement effort. Cooperation from the FBI perspective has taken on many forms:

- An office has now been established in the US Embassy in Moscow. This office, staffed by two special agents, handles strictly criminal investigations, and has promised not to become involved in the other responsibility of the FBI, counter-intelligence. At the outset, in the late summer of 1994, the office had some 30 investigative matters underway. Today, there are nearly 200 substantive investigations going on. These range from major frauds to murders, to money-laundering, to economic crime, extortion, and so forth. Surprisingly, we have found that the Russian services have become very engaged in the liaison process. They respond very well to our requests for assistance, and they have shown themselves ready to ask our agents to assist them in achieving investigations in the US. It is a rapidly-emerging partnership which today often includes Russian officers travelling to the major cities in the US, to help us in surveillance, interpretation of wire-taps, and case preparation.

- The FBI has undertaken an extensive programme of bringing ideas and methods to the Eurasian countries. Most of the US federal agencies are engaged in this effort. A special method is to send teams of investigative agents to varying regions, where they present blocks of information on methods of conducting investigations. For this purpose, agents are selected who are engaged in this type of investigation in the US, so that there is a dialogue available between them and their counterparts. In fact we unabashedly admit that the agents who do this 'training' return to the United States significantly changed. I term it as our attempts to alleviate our inherent myopia, opening the perspective of our agents, and allowing a better total understanding of the problems they are addressing. The results have been very heartening.

In addition, an active programme has been developed of inviting officers back from these various countries to share time with the FBI at the Academy at Quantico. At any time, groups of officers from the former Soviet Union are now present in the FBI classrooms and sharing their ideas and concerns. You can imagine that having Russians at the Academy took some getting used to by the older and more conservative agents. I recall one older FBI agent musing about the changing world, where a Russian police official – in uniform – would be in the same cafeteria line with him at Quantico. It is the new world order.

The FBI also initiated a major cooperative venture in Hungary. A partnership with the national police is realised in the establishment and running of the International Law Enforcement Academy (ILEA). Budapest was chosen because the Hungarians clearly showed that they wanted to be partners rather than simply hosts. The Hungarians essentially donated an existing police academy to the effort. This international academy is now in full operation. It targets the middle level managers of 23 Central and Eastern European police forces.

OTHER IMPORTANT CRIMINAL GROUPS
Colombian and Mexican traffickers.

Everyone is aware that the United States is under siege by groups from Latin America who traffic in cocaine. Suffice it to say that this is one of the most difficult tasks faced, and one of the most serious destabilising factors in the country. From a law enforcement point of view, efforts are considered moderately successful. It has become increasingly obvious that law enforcement by itself will never totally obliterate this scourge. Methods and skills have been honed, relationships between and among the various responsible US agencies have been smoothed. Relationships between law enforcement agencies and intelligence agencies have been actively addressed, which has significantly enhanced capabilities. As with many of your countries, the American intelligence agencies have been recently charged with a mission to support international law enforcement. We are in the process of quantifying that concept, and we have met with relative success to date.

Prison spawned groups.

Every country experiences difficulties with the prisoners in their prisons. We are certainly no exception. We have a long-standing phenomenon in which prisoners who become acquainted during their incarceration decide to join forces when they are released into society. These groups can be connected ethnically, religiously, or simply by happenstance.

Motor cycle gangs.

There are essentially three nationally established motor cycle gangs. Traditionally they are active in drug-trafficking – primarily amphetamines – extortion, kidnapping, and traditional violent crimes. Interestingly, the motor cycle gangs are run in the style of franchises. They are given charters by their national headquarters, and there is a loose-knit association among the various chapters, normally culminating in 'runs' which take the form of national conventions. These groups are actively franchising in Europe, and in most cases there is an ongoing dialogue with the FBI regarding them.

Urban youth gangs.

Again, I am afraid that this type of crime is something that we have exported to other countries throughout Europe. It started as a California and New York style of criminal association, and has now spread throughout the United States. The 'bloods' and the 'crips' are the best known of these gangs, and they are now virtually spread throughout the United States. Whereas ten years ago they were principally in the major cities, now they can be found also in medium-sized and small towns throughout the country. Violence is their trademark.

3. Conclusion

We Americans freely admit that we have an abundance of organised crime of all sorts in our country. It is a by-product of our very open and dynamic democratic society. The FBI sees its job as curtailing the illegal activity to the greatest possible extent, and as balancing the rights and safety of our citizens against this major influence. We are very proud of our successes, but we know that we have a long road ahead of us. We are extremely encouraged by the engagement of law enforcement agencies around the world. There is hope for the future. Our intention is to be leaders in the continuing battle, and to build partnerships with every agency with a similar mandate to ours. We are committed and moving toward the future.

14. ORGANISATIONAL CRIME IN FRANCE

J. Peduzzi and *J. Guimezanes*

1. Introduction

In the past, at the beginning of the nineteenth century, France experienced
the case of a former outlaw who joined the police. His name was François
Vidocq, a French adventurer and ex-convict who was recruited as Head of
the 'Sûreté', a department which was itself staffed by ex-prisoners. This is
one strategy to fight against crime that remained unique in our history.
Apart from this solution, the fight against crime – and especially the so-
called crime by trickery or 'white-collar' crime – undoubtedly requires a
deep knowledge of the circles in which criminals operate to their benefit.

2. The situation in France

In France, in 1995, the total number of crimes and offences was 3,665,320
for 58 million inhabitants. Thefts represented 65.50% against 9.75% as far
as economic and financial offences were concerned. The police are made
aware of crime and offences through external evidence such as breach of
the peace, lodging of complaints, accusations to the judicial authority, and
so on. In financial matters, it is more difficult to apprehend the criminal
phenomenon. There is in France, as everywhere, a significant number of
unrecorded offences, as only investigated cases are recorded as opposed to
actually committed offences.

As regards commercial law, the victim is often a legal entity represented by its dishonest leader who will not lodge a complaint against him-
self. However, in this field, direct losses are very important, and may result in serious economic difficulties such as, for instance, the collapse of a
company, which would result in redundancies and in the failure to pay
suppliers. In 1995 the damage caused by computer fraud is estimated to be
around 12 billion French Francs.

3. The Central Directorate of the Judicial Police

In France, in the beginning the training of investigators was, practical, that is on the job. The more experienced investigators taught the novices the tricks of the trade. This training was given punctually, case after case.

At the beginning of the twentieth century, as society become industrialised, there was an increasing flow of people and capital. In France, in 1907, a specialised and centralised service was created to fight the new kinds of offences committed by travelling and organised criminals, the *Contrôle Général des Recherches* (General Control of Search) and twelve regional squads of mobile police known as the Brigades du Tigre (the so-called Tiger's Squads), as they had been brought into being by Georges Clemenceau (nicknamed 'the Tiger'), Prime Minister at that time. This structure, which is now the Central Directorate of the Judicial Police, has been continuously modified to become the French leader of the fight against professional crime.

The training currently given to French investigators in order to enable them to better understand this phenomenon is basic in police academies, with a variable length of the training period according to rank (two years for commissioners and superintendents). The training is made up of by practical training courses alternating with theoretical training. This training is compulsory for all investigators.

Furthermore, there is continuous training during the whole career. A French police officer can follow courses within his service or outside, in specialised centres. These continuous training courses enable him to acquire a deeper knowledge according to his assignment (with the Judicial Police, the Urban Police Corps, or the Intelligence Services etc.).

Thus, at the Central Directorate of the Judicial Police, as regards economic and financial matters the police officer will follow specialised training courses in three sessions of ten days each. Thus he will acquire a deeper knowledge in more technical fields such as:

- money-laundering;

- the law of property and stock exchange;

- counterfeiting;

- computer fraud;

- the development of futures markets, etc.

In certain cases, he may also carry out certain tasks as an expert. A significant number of police officers are so specialised that it is not necessary to call upon external experts (such as computer engineers or senior accountants) in the framework of special investigations regarding, for instance, computer fraud, counterfeiting and accountancy.

Foreign countries are well aware of these specialists within the French police, and very frequently call upon the assistance of these 'expert police officers'. In 1995, this was the case for Estonia, Latvia, Poland, Hungary, Bulgaria, Malaysia and Gabon.

Thus, training is a vital element in the fight against crime, and especially financial crime.

4. Innovations

The priority of the Central Directorate of the Judicial Police has always been to strive for a higher level of efficiency by implementing more effective investigative techniques. It has developed these means within the Technical and Scientific Police with respect to:

- Implementation of the MORPHO system (automated fingerprint processing);

- modernisation and restructuring of the inter-regional laboratories of the Scientific Police;

- the creation of search-files for specialised squads.

The use of data-processing within the French police has rapidly become widespread, following the example of the computerisation of society. All these means are made available to the police officer investigating criminal or financial matters.

It is acknowledged that investigations carried out in connection with financial offences are essentially different from those falling within the scope of common law. The typical criminal police officer bases his investigation on a precise offence in order to ascertain the offender's identity: it is a deductive investigative process. In financial matters, however, the investigator will strive to find out, by analysing the activities of a commercial company or a venture, whether offences were committed by an already identified offender: this is an inductive investigative process. He will have to clear up the mechanisms used, in order to demonstrate the offence. Confronted with an offender who is often a prominent citizen, for example a company manager, in any case a person well-integrated into the social community, the investigator must be bright, and must have legal, technical and practical skills which allow him to complete the procedure.

5. Inter-ministerial structures and regional services

From a historical point of view, the organisation of the Central Directorate of the Judicial Police results from its adjustment to the fight against crime. Since 1907, offices have been created which are inter-ministerial structures aiming at the fight against certain kinds of aggravated crime, such as:

- Currency counterfeiting   1929

- Drugs trafficking   1953

- Trade in human beings   1958

- Organised crime   1973

- Thefts of works of art   1975

- Trafficking in arms and sensitive materials 1982

- Organised financial crime   1990

As the years went by, the 12 Mobile Squads became 20 Regional Services of Judicial Police with a wide territorial competence. This outstanding system is completed by the ever-alert intellectual curiosity of the investigator who studies and inquires new crime perspectives. Some years ago, for instance, by monitoring significant purchases of postage stamps by companies, offences of misuse of company assets were discovered, some managers bought collectable stamps among other stamps in order to make personal profit. Should privileged and mobilised observers report any unusual practice in business circles, the Judicial Police can anticipate and stop the development of new kinds of crime. This technique is also used in the fight against money-laundering.

As regards bribery, in France as elsewhere, 'cases' were often reported by the media. This insistent publicity aroused suspicions towards the political world. Most elected representatives, however, fulfil the requirements of their mandates with honesty. Nevertheless, they can be exposed to such risks as misappropriation of public funds and legal acquisition of interests. When business deals are made or public utilities commissioned, fraudulent manoeuvres may occur. To date, there is no statistical data to evaluate the importance of this phenomenon. A number of preventive measures have been recommended in this respect, which should lead to a better awareness in elected representatives concerning penalties incurred and should enable the implementation of checks on the conclusion of important deals.

6. International police cooperation

International police cooperation does exist, and has developed a great deal during the last years, but still it does not keep pace with criminal organisations. The French Police has correspondents such as:

- liaison officers;

- agencies abroad within central offices (i.e. the OCRTIS – the Central Office for the Repression of Drugs Trafficking).

The International and Technical Police Cooperation Service has sent delegates abroad who, as police officers, are privileged observers and valuable correspondents for the investigators. International relations are also strengthened by visits of experts from abroad, and during international meetings by direct contacts between police officers dealing with the same type of crime.

The International Criminal Police Organisation remains, through the National Central Bureaux, the best instrument for exchanging information. In France, this Bureau is situated within the Judicial Police department. This represents an advantage, as the requests for research or investigations are examined by a qualified officer.

The French Judicial Police also take part in several international groups, such as:

- The Financial Action Task Force (FATF), created in 1989 during the summit of the Arch, which aims at preventing the use of the banking and financial system for money-laundering operations;

- the Drugs and Organised Crime Group of the European Union.

This list is not complete, but it does reveal that France is successful in gathering as much data as possible to gain successes in the fight against organised crime.

15. THE CRIME SITUATION IN RUSSIA AND EMERGING TRENDS

V.N. Petrov

1. The general situation

An analysis of the criminal situation in the Russian Federation brings to light some positive changes in the dynamics and structure of crimes in Russia. Compared to last year, there is a certain decrease in the total number of crimes, including aggravated crimes. The number of serious crimes has decreased by 3.6%. Reference in this respect should be made to the most dangerous crimes. Thus the number of premeditated murders has decreased by 6%, and serious injuries by 12.5%. There is also a decline in robberies, burglaries, thefts and violent crimes.

A decrease in public security crime can also be discerned. The level of so-called street crime has gone down. The number of such crimes has been reduced by 22%, including premeditated murder (24%), aggravated injuries (31%), robberies (16%) and burglaries (24%). The number of serious crimes shows an increase in only one-third of the Russian Federation regions.

It should be noted that aggravated crimes still dominate within the crime structure, and comprise 57% of the total number of crimes. The amount of contract killings remains stable. One of the negative factors affecting the dynamics and structure of crimes is organised crime. In 1995 alone, 2,600 new organised criminal formations were detected.

Illegal drug-trafficking has become a serious problem. Russia has acquired the reputation of a state with favourable conditions for indigenous and international drug-traffickers, whether in trafficking itself or in drug-related money-laundering. According to expert estimates, the volume of drug-trafficking during the last year approached 3.5 million Roubles.

Juvenile delinquency has increased by 6%. It is noteworthy that there has been a 20% increase in juvenile delinquency committed by females.

Bearing in mind the current criminal situation in Russia, the Ministry of the Interior has concentrated its efforts on several aspects. First of all, we aim to further perfect detective and investigative activities relating to serious crime. In 1995, 42,500 more crimes were solved than in 1994. There has also been an improvement regarding the situation of economic crime control. The number of crimes solved in this sector has increased by 15%. The situation with regard to the reimbursement of economic crime damages, however, has worsened considerably.

One of the main stabilising factors of the operational situation is the promotion of security and public order in urban areas. Measures will also have to be taken in the view of the forthcoming presidential election in order to prevent all kinds of extremist activity.

2. Crime geography

The concentration of activities around centres of financial capital also influenced the geographic aspect of crime. The criminal situation was more intense in the regions with a high level of business and investment activity, including investment in illegal assets. Favourable conditions for a quick turnover and high profit possibilities are important factors here. The main areas of activity of criminal groups continued to be the big economic and financial centres and regions, economic free-zones, border territories and transport routes.

3. Review of the situation by the types of registered offences

Violent crimes

Within the violent crime structure, a number of negative trends have emerged. One of these trends is a significant shift in the motivation of types of crime such as premeditated crimes and aggravated assault. Whereas a large number of these crimes were previously committed spontaneously, on routine grounds, at present there are many meticulously organised offences among such crimes.

Property crime

The number of crimes against property has increased by 2.8%, and reached a level of 1.665 million offences (60.4% of all registered offences). According to expert evaluations, the most destructive factor, influencing both society and the criminal situation in the country, was the immense concentration of capital and means of production in the hands of some individuals.

Economic crime

Misappropriation of state property in the course of privatisation and abuse in its administration, as well as the illegal redistribution of the Gross National Product in favour of criminal structures, were the main features of the criminal process in the economy of Russia in 1995. This occurred mainly through criminal schemes in the credit, financial and foreign economic spheres, and in currency and consumer markets.

There were 211,826 registered economic offences in 1995, i.e. 7.7% of the total number of offences. Almost half of the registered economic crime cases fall within the category of misappropriation. This comprises two-thirds of the material losses caused by economic crimes. This emerging possibility to concentrate a significant part of property in private businesses stimulated offences based on selfish motivations, and caused the appearance of new types of crime not typical for the previous years, such as large-scale fraud caused by various financial institutions, to the detriment of investors

Organised crime

Just as in the previous years, a major part of the shadow capital concentrated in the criminal sphere was used for the reproduction of crime on a wider scale. Along with murder, violent theft, and qualified extortion, as characteristic features of organised crime, the country also saw continuing active integration into the economic sector, with the aim of obtaining enormous, illegal, profits.

In order to achieve their goals, criminal groups, in addition to employing the tactic of terror, actively use bribes to corrupt state officials. Operational data indicates that corrupt officials cooperate with at least every tenth organised criminal group.

In the course of 1995, 2,800 criminal leaders and active members of those groups were sentenced. 4,800 firearms, financial and other assets, amounting to more than 501 billion roubles, foreign currency (128.8 million US dollars) and around 1,100 vehicles were seized.

Drugs

In the last year, the drug situation continued to deteriorate. Drug abuse has grown markedly, involving hundreds of thousands of new drug addicts, primarily juveniles. It resulted in the growth of illegal drug-trafficking and further developments regarding the integration process of the Russian drug dealers into the system of international drug-trafficking.

The total number of registered drug-related offences has increased by 6.7% and reached the figure of 79,800. 25,000 illegal drug plantations, including 800 poppy plantations, were destroyed. 15.4 tons of narcotic drugs and 4.3 tons of drugs containing herbs (marihuana) were seized.

4. Emerging trends in the development of crime in 1996

Taking into account the fact that criminality can be characterised as a social phenomenon with a high ineptness, it is worth noticing that the main developments in the crime situation are not likely to change significantly. Stable factors arising from drastic changes in the economic, political and social sectors are likely to influence the criminal situation continuously.

1996 will most probably be marked by an aggravated competition for property, characterised by armed clashes and violent seizures or destruction of assets. The clash of selfish interests with the beginning of a new stage of revision of zones of influence between criminal structures, together with criminal penetration into the sphere of the most profitable projects of the economy, can become a powerful catalyst in worsening this country's criminal situation.

Shadow businesses in the credit and financial sphere, and investment charity funds, are likely to grow. There will be a rise in the number of fraud schemes with bank guarantees, payment cards, financial embezzlement at banks by means of computer-related crime. It can be expected that the influence of organised crime, not only within CIS-countries but also within other countries will increase, as will the laundering of criminal assets abroad. International criminal economic and multi-purpose structures will be more active in the spheres of the illegal export of precious and non-ferrous metals and other raw materials.

In making a prognosis on the growth of organised crime, it is worth mentioning further intensive consolidation of the criminal world. Shadow transitional and interregional organised crime communities will continue to form. This will provide huge, unprecedented bank fraud schemes, large-scale financial embezzlement, misappropriation of assets, massive corruption of state officials and an increase in control over the most profitable branches of the economy.

It is also expected that new *modus operandi* of committing crime will appear, and there will be a transition from extortion in relation to individual businessmen, to 'long-lasting agreements' with the business sector on the payment of fixed 'contributions'.

The huge financial means possessed by criminal groups will probably be used not only to bribe state and public officials and to create a corrupt layer in all branches of the state apparatus, thus providing a cover for criminal activities. It will also probably be used to further counter the law enforcement system, exerting pressure on the participants in the law enforcement process.

16. SUPRANATIONAL POLICE-TRAINING

S. Pintèr

1. Introduction: quantitative and qualitative data

Crime in Hungary increased at a moderate rate between 1984 and 1988, but from 1988 until 1991 the increase took place at a higher pace. The annual 25–48% increase rose from a total of 150,000 criminal cases in 1988 to a peak of 447,000 cases in 1992. After a temporary decline and stagnation in the number of cases of crime, we are now, in the middle of the current decade, at the figure of 502,000 criminal offences a year, which means 4,900 per 100,000 population.

Besides the increase in figures, qualitative changes have also taken place. In addition to the common criminal offences and the group of criminals living on occasional criminal activities, groups using methods of organised crime, and organised criminal groups or gangs have emerged.

The transition of government that took place in the years 1989–1990, the emergence of the market economy and privatisation, have elevated investments in business sectors promising extra profits in the sphere of organised crime endeavours.

The organised criminal social layer, specialised in targeting entrepreneurs and investors inexperienced in the area of market economy, has caused extremely severe damage. Through a series of fraudulent activities, material losses have been inflicted worth nearly 37,000,000 ECU, making almost 100,000 victims, whose confidence in the market economy is now severely undermined.

The organised criminal elements are continually making attempts at penetrating the state administration, the political and economic sectors, or the organisations playing an important part in these sectors, respectively.

The disappearance of borders also made room for an almost unimpeded movement of criminals, and to their 'exchanges of experience'.

Of the traditional forms of perpetration of crimes, the greatest concern is caused by car thefts and related criminal acts (sale of stolen vehicles, cross-border transport of stolen vehicles), and also by the smuggling of and trafficking in illicit drugs, which is growing steadily. We perceive ever more indications of illegal gun-running and trafficking in nuclear material.

2. New perspectives for organised and organisational crime

The trend described above, which in many countries of the world has been a well-known phenomenon for a long time, became a reality – for law enforcement agencies and criminals alike – in Hungary and the former communist countries after the transition in government. The conditions of the former social and economic structures did not allow for the strengthening of endeavours contrary to the central political will. Thus the chance for someone not supported by the official ideology and by the official politicians to achieve anything in the political or economic sphere was indeed rather minimal.

In the period after the transition of government, as an undesirable spin-off of the expansion of democracy, organised crime grew stronger. Various criminal groups, organisations of the underworld at first mainly employed intimidation methods. Our colleagues in the state administration and law enforcement agencies who were standing in their way often received threats in which they themselves or members of their family were endangered. The fiasco of this method – although at present it is still used from time to time – has led to the situation that so-called organisational crime has now become more typical in our country. It should be stated right at the beginning that only extremely rarely is organisational crime limited to local targets, it usually assumes regional and national significance, and what is more, it often has international implications. It is therefore expedient to handle issues of organised and organisational crime together.

3. Responses of law enforcement

The Hungarian National Police have not acquiesced in the endeavours of organised crime and have taken the following steps to manage the situation that has evolved, and to prevent more serious problems:

- bilateral agreements have been agreed upon with eleven countries for purposes of cooperation in the field of combating organised crime, terrorism and illicit drug-trafficking;

- study tours have been organised to countries of the European Community and the United States of America;

- organisational changes have been implemented. The Organised Crime Service Branch has been established, which not only carries out operational work, but also has national competence in coordinating the direction of specialised law enforcement actions against organised crime;

- amendments of preventive legal regulations have been initiated, especially regarding the detection of organised crime, organisational crime and drug-related crime. Well-tried regulations of Western Europe have been taken into account in this respect.

Our own experiences have underlined the importance of cooperation within the European Union in the internal and justice areas, especially concerning the involvement of the Central and East-European associated countries. The fight against organised crime, that increasingly takes on international dimensions and has grown stronger all over Europe, can only be successful through an all-European joining of forces.

4. Conditions favourable to organised and organisational crime

We have made an inventory of the conditions that have facilitated the sudden advance of international and organisational crime in Hungary and in our region, and of those that have hindered national police forces from being successful in combating them. Of these conditions, the following can be considered to be of outstanding significance:

Conditions facilitating international and organisational crime on the criminals' (perpetrators') side:

- the criminals' freedom of movement across borders;
- the establishment of personal contacts between international criminals (criminal groups being organised on the basis of clans and ethnic relationships);
- a rapid spread of new methods and means of criminal activities;
- the use, investment and laundering of money obtained through the perpetration of crime in other countries;
- the transition of stolen goods, their circulation in other countries;
- the opportunity to escape prosecution by resettling in a foreign country or by continuous travelling from one country to the other;
- criminals' showdowns and vendettas committed across the borders;
- masterminding and mounting criminal acts (terrorist acts) from a foreign country;

- the low income level of public servants in the former communist countries;

- the rapid growth of differences in property status of the population in the former communist countries, the appearance, in certain individuals, of the desire to get rich quick;

- the partial or total disintegration of the former state security, police and home-defence agencies and organisations in several countries (some of the former employees of these agencies have gone over to the criminals' side);

- the almost baffling mushrooming of international business enterprises;

- the unclear legal status of the emerging market economy.

Conditions facilitating international and organisational crime
on the police (law enforcement) side:

- the different degrees of readiness of national police forces to cooperate;

- inadequate knowledge of each other's legal system, organisational structure and functional-operational procedures;

- traditional agreements on legal assistance that lag behind the requirements of up-to-date law enforcement;

- problems of communication:
  - ◆ human factors (language barriers, lack of personal contacts)
  - ◆ technical equipment (lack of compatibility of information system equipment);

- lack of uniformity of terms (the same term has different meanings in the different police forces);

- the different features of the warrant systems;

- obstacles created by data protection;

- the differences in the current level of training;

- the slow spread of effective means and methods of law enforcement;

- the administrative, bureaucratic and 'juridical' obstacles of operational contacts;

- the difference of national documents issued for the same purpose, lack of standardisation and lack of knowledge of formal requirements;

- partly or totally limited authority/powers in a foreign country;

- ill-preparedness for the rapid appearance of international organised crime and its *modus operandi*;

- wrong attitudes carried over from the period preceding the transition of government, which are difficult to change, specially the attitude that certain organisations and individuals were 'inaccessible' or 'untouchable' for the police.

5. Factors facilitating international criminal prosecution and cooperation

Not only negative features were identified during these analytic efforts, components were also discovered which prevail almost automatically and which could be employed for the purposes of cooperation.

The following factors will facilitate the strengthening of relations between the police forces of different countries:

- defining a common goal;

- finding a common basis for the criminal sciences;

- development of the sciences that will create an opportunity to employ unified means and methods of criminal/forensic technology;

- achieving similarity of principles of criminal methodology and criminal tactics;

- up-to-date police officer training;

- the experience gained from the agreements concluded so far, and from the occasional cooperative efforts;

- similarities in the geo-political situation and historical background.

6. The need for improving police education and training

6.1. NATIONAL AND INTERNATIONAL TRAINING

It is our conviction that the greatest achievement with the least effort can be made in the area of police officer training, and especially with regard to international police training. This follows from the fact that it seems to be from within the framework of an educational institution that information and instruction on legal systems, historical and professional traditions, and principles of international cooperation is easiest to acquire.

Thinking together will be facilitated by an organisational and structural similarity of police academies and training institutes and by similar methods of teaching the police profession. In this area, initial experience was gained abroad, where we could participate in national law enforcement education systems provided for by nations that granted assistance to Hungary.

First we implemented training reform for the Hungarian National Police. As of now, we provide two-year intermediate level training for police-functionaries, and a three-year college level training for officers, both qualifications being acknowledged by the state.

Our experience shows that international obligations can only be met successfully if a high standard of national basic training is complemented with postgraduate international training. Only initial, basic level police training commenced abroad will not be enough to be successful. Mastering and later applying in practice the basic terminology in the mother tongue and in one's own country will create a much firmer basis for, and security of, police action than if the same learning process had taken place in a foreign country. Learning about the legal system and regulations first, especially if these differ from the principles to be implemented in the day-to-day working environment, can cause serious confusion at critical moments. The significance of foreign or international law enforcement training should especially be directed at personnel who already have professional qualifications. What is more, in some duties and positions we consider this to be indispensable.

6.2. THE CENTRAL EUROPEAN POLICE ACADEMY

To date, Hungary already operates and maintains several schools and training courses that are attended by students from foreign countries.

Mention must first be made of the Central European Police Academy. The idea of establishing such an academy originated as early as 1991. The ministers of the interior of Austria and Hungary signed a Memorandum of Understanding in March 1992, as a result of which the joint further training of Austrian and Hungarian police officers started in that same year. On the basis of favourable initial experiences, the initiative was soon joined by the Czech, Polish, Slovak and Slovenian Police Forces, to be followed by Germany in 1994. The Central European Police Academy has become a forum of further training, conducted in German, where police officers already in possession of practical experience and expertise can deepen their knowledge and share their experience in combating cross-border organised crime. Themes dealt with first of all are phenomena such as terrorism, illegal drug-trafficking, illegal gun-running, organisational crime, and also economic and environmental crime.

The success of the Academy is guaranteed by the following facts:

- it does not function in a location tied to one specific city;

- the specific features of several countries can be studied in one course;

- it can provide firm legal and methodological foundations in international cooperation;

- it provides not only theoretical knowledge, but also information that can be utilised in practical field work;

- it establishes invaluable personal and fraternal relationships;

- it enhances trust and confidence in one another, and thereby quickens the flow of information;

- it increases the sense of responsibility.

The popularity of the Central European Police Academy can be illustrated by the fact that in the past five years, 1,113 students from 7 countries have graduated from its training courses. In 1996, Switzerland also joined this form of further training. According to the arrangements made, Swiss colleagues will participate in the common efforts from next year onwards. Still, it would be a mistake for any one country to vindicate the authorship of these successes, because the achievements are to the accumulated credit of all contributing nations.

6.3. THE INTERNATIONAL LAW ENFORCEMENT ACADEMY

Great satisfaction is also derived from another form of international police and law enforcement cooperation: the International Law Enforcement Academy (ILEA), which extends not only across borders of countries, but also of continents. This initiative was also supported by the US Government, which later assisted in establishing and maintaining the institution.

The idea of establishing such an academy first cropped up in 1994, during the visit to Budapest of Mr. Louis Freeh, Director of the FBI. After several discussions, and precise coordination requiring the input of 16 countries, we together elaborated the basic principles and educational curricula acceptable for all concerned. As a result of these concerted efforts, the doors of the Academy could be opened on 24 April 1995, the National Police Day in Hungary.

The basic mission of the new international educational institution is to help middle level managers of the Central European police forces' organisations responsible for dealing with organised crime, to make their work as successful as possible. The functioning of the Academy is supported not only by the United States and Canada, but also by almost all West European countries. As a result, it has become possible for 25 police forces of Eastern Europe to take advantage of the opportunities offered by the Academy. We are proud to be able to host this Academy. The ILEA is under the direction of an American director, who is supported by four experts. The instructors are selected from experts from the FBI, the Drug Enforcement Administration (DEA) and other American, Canadian and West European law enforcement agencies. Students are selected for each session from three different countries. Until the renovation of the Academy facilities is completed, ten students from each of these three countries (a total of 30) can study at the academy. After the renovation has been completed, sixteen students from each of the three countries, plus two Hungarian students, can attend. A session lasts 8 weeks. The first session was attended by Czech, Polish and Hungarian police officers.

The following advantages of the ILEA should be highlighted:

- training is conducted in the students' mother tongue (through simultaneous translation);

- the curriculum introduces decades of experience of the law enforcement agencies;

- working in advanced democracies;

- it lays the foundation for a Central European Academic Centre of Police;

- it establishes personal relationships between East European police officers;

- it facilitates and encourages the resolution of tensions between different peoples of the region;

- it offers the opportunity to learn and practise a foreign language;

- it encourages the collective thinking process of the region's police forces finding themselves in similar situations;

- it promotes the introduction of uniform methods and means;

- the conferences organised by the Academy are suitable for providing a meeting and discussion forum for ministers, and chiefs of national police forces;

- it can deal with the following issues with the latest and most up-to-date information:
    combating organised crime
    combating drug-related crime and illegal sales of arms;
    dealing with organisational crime;
    issues of police ethics;
    human rights;
    tasks of the police in disaster, hostage-taking, kidnap situations;
    the police officer's physical condition (fitness programme);
    analysis of specific cases of crime.

Naturally, as with all beginnings, the launching of the ILEA was a difficult task, but, with a common resolve, all obstacles have been removed and the work continues to achieve the greatest possible efficiency. The initial experiences brought several problems to the fore, which were discussed with our American partners. It was through a joint decision that the following was agreed upon:

- an entrance examination should be developed for the applicants;

- the preparedness, qualifications and spheres of interest of students in the same group should be as uniform as possible;

- the curriculum and presentations should be better adapted to the students.

6.4. POLICE TRAINING AND ORGANISATIONAL CRIME

The need to deal with organisational crime, the importance of handling the issue, was touched upon here with regard to the role of international educational institutions. Naturally, the same principles are expressed in the curricula of the educational institutions of the Hungarian National Police.

Still the role of educational institutes in dealing with organisational crime is limited. The problem is beyond what can be resolved by police means and methods alone, although no results can be achieved without them. Suffice it to say that it is hardly possible to launder hundreds of millions of dollars annually (emanating, for instance, from illegal drug-trafficking) without several banks and financial institutions being interested in it. It would, however, be a grave mistake not to prepare junior officers for the existence of organisational crime or the importance of prosecuting it, for the dangers that await police officers. Therefore the following issues should be included in the curricula of the educational institutions:

- information on the major goals of organisational crime, the most threatened, so-called 'target organisations', should become available;
- lawful, presentable aspirations of organised crime should be determined;
- methods of infiltrating target organisations must be developed;
- specific cases should be analysed.

The first four issues will be outlined here, with emphasis at the same time that they must be dealt with in greater detail in the course of institutional training.

Our experience tells us that organisational crime intends to achieve the following aims in relation to the target organisation:

- influencing or enforcing decisions in a manner favourable for itself;
- acquisition of data and information within its sphere of interest;
- acquisition of documents or means facilitating its activities, or obtaining precursor materials necessary for the production of such documents (vehicle registration documents, printing clichés, arms, etc.);
- laundering of ill-gotten money;
- at least partial legalisation of criminal activities;
- establishing international criminal contacts and maintaining such relationships;
- training and education of its own 'experts';
- compromising and provoking or possibly bribing directors and members of official organisations taking actions against them;
- elimination of lawful or illegal rivals.

Organised crime prefers to select as target organisations:

- police and border guard organisations;

- customs and internal revenue services;
- military organisations;
- civilian secret services (intelligence agencies);
- courts of justice, prosecutors' offices;
- financial institutions;
- printed and electronic press;
- political parties;
- travel agencies;
- commercial and transportation companies;
- joint stock companies with significant incomes.

At the same time, one can also observe that organised crime, besides operating within or with the help of lawful enterprises and companies, is often involved in activities with apparently good intentions. Still, these activities often are closely related to arriving at illegal aims. For instance:

- providing support for political campaigns;
- establishment of foundations;
- providing support for the arts and sports;
- providing support for charitable causes or charity organisations.

In most cases, politicians, scientists, artists and sportsmen and women do not have the slightest idea where the money awarded to them really comes from. Thus their name is used for events, where the only part they are really meant to play is to lend legitimacy to the programme and provide publicity for otherwise undeserving individuals.

As main methods of infiltration, the following can be mentioned:

- gaining information about former and active, and now often impecunious, state security officers of the former communist countries in order to revive their old contacts;
- blackmailing and bribing individuals working in target organisations;
- inserting individuals, selected from their own criminal circles, into the target organisation;

- picking out talented young men, supporting them, placing them in key positions, and finally 'handing in the bill';

- establishing confidential relationships with persons working in target organisations, or with their relatives and friends;

- recruiting persons who were previously discharged from a target organisation on any ground, or winning over a former employee of the target organisation who voluntarily left it, to revive their old contacts.

All issues mentioned should be considered to be very important within training programmes, but infiltration into target organisations is one of the most important issues here. For this trend already presents a real danger for new colleagues as well. That is why it is the responsibility of the schools to provide enhanced protection of the students against the aspirations of organisational crime.

7. Conclusion

I would like to list below some of our specific plans related to CEPA and ILEA:

- enhancement of practical training and of introduction to national idiosyncrasies;

- elaboration of methods that accelerate international cooperation and make it safe;

- enlargement of the national academic staff;

- publication of multilingual textbooks, videos and teaching aids;

- increase the number of participating countries and students attending, and making this possible by extending the current educational facility;

- further training of border law enforcement and traffic law enforcement officers at the CEPA.

Experience gained so far in the national and international education and training conducted at the institutions of the Hungarian National Police justifies the following general proposals. For purposes of the future efficiency of police education it would be necessary to implement international police education in a three-level system. The three levels are:

An academic type of further training.

1. Further training for senior executives (commanders).

2. Further training for field officers.

Within this system, courses with different contents and duration would be conducted, such as:

a.) Courses providing special (specialised) new knowledge.

b.) Refresher courses, with an extension of knowledge, also from the international perspective.

c.) Courses analysing police methods and measures used in specific major or special cases.

We foresee the three levels of education in the following arrangement: the first would admit colleagues with a high level of theoretical and practical knowledge, who, after the analysis of international experience, would discuss concepts of scientific-academic value, and would adopt them for purposes of future cooperation.

The second level would involve getting together mainly middle and top level executives from criminal investigation and public safety speciality fields. They would be given assistance primarily in short-term planning and in executing their day-to-day tasks.

The third level would involve basically crime officers, but also public safety officers, interfacing with the citizens on a daily basis, i.e. uniformed street police officers who would get together. This form of further training may seem unrealistic today, because the conditions for it in fact do not yet exist. A citizen of a Europe that is to be unified in the future, however, has every right to expect to feel safe and to be safe. No matter which country he goes to on the continent, he expects to be able to turn to an officer of the national police in confidence, and he expects the procedures of the authorities to be of virtually the same standard as those in his own country. The methods used should strengthen a feeling of mutual respect, rather than a feeling of defencelessness.

In approving of our intentions and proposals, the Minister of the Interior of the Republic of Hungary supports our endeavours to make Budapest and Hungary, respectively, provide more venues for international police training, first and foremost for the police officers of Central and East Europe.

We are ready to support similar aspirations of other countries, because we are convinced that in order to create a unified Europe, the unified approach, just as the readiness of law enforcement agencies and organisations to cooperate, is indispensable.

17. EPILOGUE

B. Hoogenboom and M.J. Meiboom

The 13th European IACP Conference carried the challenging title **'Policing the Future'** and such a title obviously begs the questions as to whether this conference dealt with 'policing' and the 'future' and, if so, based on which (or even whose) paradigms?

The answer to these questions cannot be given unequivocally. Yes: the conference dealt with the topics mentioned. And no: it was not always made clear what the point of departure was, or what paradigms were used.

All contributors have touched upon issues in policing. Both on national and international levels policing is undergoing drastic changes. Policing is continuously adapting itself to changes in society and to new forms of crime. It is therefore heartening to see that a number of contributions have undertaken forays into the next millennium. The sum of the forays, however, does not present us with a coherent or cohesive picture of what that millennium has in store for policing.

There seems to be a broad consensus on the need to integrate the former Eastern European countries into already existing democratic police structures. But form and contents do not always agree.

If we scratch the surface of consensus we find some disharmony. Of course, the Chief Constables of the Hungarian, Dutch and American police forces agree on the need to have the police working closer to and with people they are supposed to protect. And it is to be expected that there are nuances in their approach as they stem from different cultures and have different political and sociological backgrounds. But what sort of curriculum will have to developed in international training programmes? What quality standards will have to be set, and by whom? What sort of international standards have to be developed for crime analysis? How do we overcome the fragmentation of definitions? Although on the surface there would appear to be consensus on concepts such as community policing, financial investigation, international training and organised crime, a number of contributions offer different historical developments, political cultures, training levels and working experiences which, so it would seem, deeply affect interpretation and contents. The shadow of the biblical Tower of Babylon still looms over international police cooperation.

But a lot of ground has been covered. There is an evident need to discuss contents in the near future. The IACP conferences offer one of the forums to stimulate this. In retrospect, it is rather simple to play devil's advocate, but in this case the exercise seems to be worthwhile as it provides new 'food for thought'. The conference has fulfilled a number of needs. It has given participants an opportunity to share experiences and views, discuss new developments and basically learn from each other. But, slipping into our devil's advocate role, we would like to point to a number of issues essential to the future of policing.

First and foremost, policing is discussed within the framework of the state monopoly on violence. It is in that context, from those structural confines if you will, that we are informed about community policing, organisational police structures, the rule of law and organisational crime.

To a certain extent this context is limited. As society transforms from an industrial society into an information society, the police function will inevitably have to be redefined. Policing in the industrial society was an answer to public order problems and crime typical of society at the time. Organisational structures, recruitment, training, leadership and culture of policing are a product of the industrial society.

With the advent of the information society, however, policing in society becomes more fragmented. The rise of private security is especially noteworthy in this respect. Public order, surveillance and even the investigative process are undergoing privatisation. Public order problems nowadays also occur in the largely private domain. Shopping malls, industrial and residential areas have their private police forces or at best some form of public-private partnerships. The business community hires private investigators, in insurance fraud cases and to combat all sorts of internal fraudulent behaviour.

Public order in the information society stretches itself into Cyberspace. As we communicate with each other on the information highway and make use of the Internet and other on-line forms of communication we will have to be increasingly aware of the flip-side of this late 20th century coin. However fascinated we are with the Internet, it is also the home of those elements that we, up to now at least, have agreed are less desirable (and in some countries even forbidden by law) such as fascist, neo-nazis groups, child pornographers and the site for the Anarchist Cookbook.

Privatisation and technological innovation are but a few of the fundamental challenges to policing and its traditional framework. A number of themes addressed at the conference are a product of the 'industrial mind'.

To fully address policing the future, new questions have to be raised in following conferences because, both on a strategic and operational level, new forms of partnership, but also of new competition are emerging. We will have to explore the concept of public-private partnership. As we will have to realise that the issue of what some commentators in this book call the multi-agency approach needs new strategic management capacities.

On an operational level, the blurring of the lines between underworld and business world and organised crime, white-collar crime and organisational crime has serious implications for crime analysis and tactical operations, both organisationally as well as financially. The complexity of frauds and international money-laundering schemes must have consequences for the recruitment and training of police officers.

Nevertheless, we are convinced that this conference is a step in the right direction. As you know, an old Chinese proverb says: 'The road to the future starts with the first step'. Together we must take that first step and together, inevitably, we will succeed.